ANGER MANAGEMENT
WORKBOOK FOR KIDS

Social skills activities for kids: 100 fun activities for Talking, Listener, and Understand. Coping Skills to Overcome Anxiety and Help About Emotions and Anger Management.

Richard Kim

Table of Contents

INTRODUCTION

The latest findings by a team of researchers at Georgia School of Medicine cannot surprise parents reading this. The first of these studies published in November issue of the medical journal Pediatric Exercise Science, which focuses on our perception of childhood exercise, found that aerobics appears to have a significant impact on childhood frustration.

Children's anger management is harder to handle than ever since children like to learn by looking at others. And today there are many negative or dubious idols which children want to equalize with, because of the Internet, TV, computers and video games. Children cannot be taught how to control and manage their rage.

Child anger management is an important topic. Teenage years are critical to children's development. Sadly, these are the years in which children experience some of their most difficult meetings. This precise time in the life of a child will lead them in many directions, some not so good. Teenagers often drop out when they have to house unpleasant circumstances. A careless perspective is common in many teenagers. If young people turn to emotions of wrath and begin to act, it may be time to seek anger for them.

Chapter one: What Is Anger Management?

Whether you're someone who have anger or just curious, you might wonder.

What's the management anger?

The sentence is casually thrown around, but in fact, it is a severe treatment that can help people to manage their intense emotions, especially their rage.

The majority of psychological experts would define wrath management as recognition and control of your wrath. It's not just something that's done once.

If you have a problem with anger, you will have to deal with this problem for the rest of your life. When left untreated, a long list of financial, physical, mental, and emotional issues will inevitably be brought on.

The first aspect of wrath management describes the problem of wrath that you or your beloved may have. From time to time, most people become angry; anger is a healthy and normal emotion.

It's quite natural to feel angry if somebody disappoints you, or if you think that you have no control over a terrible situation or are taking advantage of it. Most of the people were prepared to deal with this rage positively and healthily.

People who need anger control have a problem with How to react to the feeling of anger. It turns into uncontrollable something, often harming or threatening itself or others, instead of handling it properly.

Unmanaged anger can lead to depression, anxiety, suicide, and other harm.

You will understand the need by recognizing what anger management is. If you have a problem checking how you feel, especially if you are angry, you may have a few issues.

If you are unable to overcome something or something wrong, or you tend to blow seemingly small problems into huge problems, you could have an anger problem.

If you are aggressive or physically or verbally threatening, you know that you need help with anger management techniques.

Those with anger management problems could also have difficulty maintaining healthy relationships. If you have an issue of resentment, you are very likely not to treat people always well or equally.

Most people who have a difficult time with anger alienate their friends and family. You and the propensity to participate in confrontations, debates, or combat will be avoided.

Take a look at your life and understand how it could impact frustration. If you want to add more meaningful relationships and positive experiences into your life but don't know, because you're always mad, then it's time to manage yourself.

There are many opportunities to benefit from treatment options. You can do this yourself; you can use books and other printed multimedia, and visual content. Seek anything that explores the control of frustration and how it can work for you.

You can learn about experts in the field of mental health, visit websites, and sign up online for newsletters and other info. Talking about rage and how it affects you is the first big step to managing the issue.

A professional therapist or consultant is a good idea. You should talk about what makes you mad, how you respond, and how you want to act.

A therapist will ask you about your history, particularly how you have behaved like a child, how you grew up, and if you were subjected to a lot of untouched wrath as a child.

This has a profound effect on your emotional and mental health today. The therapist will show you some excellent methods in anger management and help you to track how you do with various strategies and resources.

Another great way to deal with your anger is by supporting groups. Speaking with others with anger issues is a great way to deal with the control of anger and how to use it for your good.

You can share your own stories and listen to other people's stories. Many items may sound familiar to you, and you will be able to find comfort by not being alone.

You'll even learn some brilliant anger management tricks, and you can also share your own.

If you or someone you know has emotional problems resulting from anger problems, recognize the problem. You can't help until you realize that something needs to be done to embrace a healthy and productive life.

Don't ignore the problem or frustration that might lurk. Start by educating yourself about the management of anger so that you can choose the best tools for your life.

Anger Management for Kids

Anger-it's a part of life, and everyone feels it. Wrath isn't a negative emotion. We should not try to suppress or bury it, which only reinforces and ferociousness. However, we must understand, practice, and teach our kids valuable anger management skills to learn to deal with anger at an early stage. In our schools, homes, and societies, we have seen the devastating effects of the marginalized rage. Let us learn to handle it efficiently now so that there are no odd moments in the life of your family.

Recognize the rage and the right of your child to be angry. You don't want to know if you're upset that you have no right to be angry or to "stop doing so." You want to show your frustration because deep inside you is a sense of injustice. Anger often has pain or fear at heart. The source of anger comes from the sense that love is somehow rejected. His clothes can vary. You may think that you have a plausible reason for anger at first sight- but underneath that rage is always a secret fear or pain.

Through talking out, help your child dig into this fear or pain. Get to the root of the problem. Don't shout back if your child screams; just stay still and hear the situation calmly. Certainly, don't allow your child to harm your dad, but recognize that a few lines of the explosion are sometimes necessary to prevent the cork from popping. Take a deep breath and think about it.

Let your child know that anger is all right. Don't try and stop it, just help your child learn to talk and to let her know that, as any caring person would do, you will always listen. Most of the time, it just spreads the rage, even if you have several opportunities to return to the subject. Continue to work on it until it is solved, always caring, kind, and respectful.

Model the child's acceptable anger management. Sometimes we all get mad. When you feel angry, take a deep breath and breathe deeply, concentrate, and then explain why you are angry. In fact, the more natural it is, the more you practice it. Don't think if you get upset, and you're a bad parent or a bad example. Children need appropriate emotional models, and if you cover up rage or try to hide it, your child will feel that anyway. Be frank, transparent, and learn to grow out of all experiences and emotions.

The keys to healthy relationships are friendliness and loyalty. When partnerships are not founded on respect and kindness; therefore, wrath will occur. Help your child understand all relationships in this reality.

Even if your child doesn't like someone, especially, it is essential to be as polite and kind as possible. Where there is a lack of basic kindness and respect, problems arise.

You may not always agree with your child or even agree to some choices. Nonetheless, as long as your child is kind and polite and understands who he or she is, the problems of wrath can and will be diffused. Note that you don't need to accept your child as an adult necessarily. Nevertheless, you must accept who your child is. Acceptance is essential, even if you disagree. Your child is her own individual, and several parents spend many years realizing that acceptance is the basis. Disagreement is all right; disagreement is not.

Share how you manage your anger with your child. You can use prayer, meditation, deep respiration, physical exercise, and talk to help release frustration. Prayer and meditation are medium-to-long-term solutions, while deep breathing, exercise, and chat are quick and short-term remedies to spread the immediate wrath. My 10- Year-old son learns deep breathing was of particular benefit before discussing the situation, then explaining his views. He is using the priesthood to focus on himself and feels more equilibrated and can deal more efficiently with his fluctuating emotions. He made a poster for his room a while back, which reads, "If I get too mad, I go away from things." It helped remind him to take a breather and cool off when necessary.

Often kids don't seem to know why they're so mad. We can experience an accumulation of frustration because of seemingly trivial problems. By being a loving parent who supports and seeing past anger behavior, your child can deal with these little issues at a time. Furthermore, if you spend time with your child just asking her to "feel the anger" and discuss it calmly, sadness will often come, and you will explore it together. Crossing the wrath layers can often feel like peeling an onion, but wrath is sometimes the same. Only start to peel. Stick with her through the tears, the cries, the annoys, and let her know that no matter what, you embrace her and love her.

You're essentially a model for your kids. Your child will also express your anger in undesirable ways. Use your tools to manage anger as you teach them. You want to teach your child even to deal with small problems so that wrath doesn't become the norm or becomes deeply rooted as an adolescent. Of course, you can deal with all sorts of rage as a loving parent by reverting to these values, but early intervention is the best thing. Stay calm and reflect on your job as a guide and instructor rather than being upset with any situation personally. Become an observer and an assistant.

In the end, true love involves a personal commitment to each other through simple and difficult pieces. Wrath is an emotion that must not be the worst place for a person. Respire profoundly and use compassion, respect, and kindness to restore rage and create a healthy family relationship.

Anger Management Techniques and Tips

What is anger is a term for the emotional aspect of aggression as a fundamental element of stress in animals that is "provoked" by a perceived aggravating stimulus, which also aggravates and threatens violence? Mild forms of a cold typically call themselves "distress," "displeasure," or "irritation," whereas "anger" refers to an extreme degree of coldness associated with a lack of calmness or control (in the case of human behavior).

Throughout modern society, rage is perceived as a reaction to annoyance, danger, infringement, or failure, which is childish or uncivilized. Conversely, it is more socially acceptable to keep calm, cool, or turn the other cheek. This conditioning may trigger insufficient manifestations of Wrath, such as uncontrolled and aggressive outbursts or misdirected Wrath, or, at the other extreme, repressive (or total) feelings of Wrath, when those sensations are the appropriate reaction. Furthermore, rage continually "boiled up" may cause persisting violent thoughts or hallucinations or even physical symptoms such as headaches, ulcers, or high blood pressure.

Anger Side Effects Anger can exacerbate many problems in mental health. Anger is capable of causing depression. People who are depressed don't usually care about themselves. We engage in self-destructive practices such as drinking too much, smoking, excessive consumption, taking risks, and not looking after their finances. Depressed individuals have less time, less appetite, and need more sleep. Their success will decrease, and their relationships will deteriorate.

Some conclude that depression is simply inwardly wrathful. The explanation for this theory is that many depressed individuals respond to stress by their anger as a reaction to physical or emotional abuse or neglect from parents and parents. After a while, coping mechanisms become patterns which they use indiscriminately when they encounter failure or frustration.

Depressive individuals tend to grow up believing that if they are injured or harmed, only two options are available which blame themselves and deny their guilt. One side effect of the depressive denial of rage is that their relationships with individuals are often unpleasant and do not encounter the' breaks' that other people seem to experience. We may not earn promotions, social invites, or affection because most people do not want to spend time with depressed people at home or work. The side effect of Wrath is that obsessions, phobias, and addictions can be exacerbated.

Obsessions and phobia arise from situations where we feel either losing control of ourselves or of the world around us, for one reason or another. Irritation can also drive manic patterns. Most people who can not express their anger let it go in furious action. Sometimes this activity breaks and leads to clinical depression or even bipolar disorder.

Wrath can also fan fear and discrimination, even in normal everyday circumstances. People tend passively or actively to express their anger through their underlying "flight," which is repression and denial of anger. Aggressive behavior is related to' battle' reaction and the use of verbal and physical aggression to threaten and harm others.

Symptoms of wrath Anger could be of one of two principal types: passive Wrath and aggressive Wrath. Both forms of cold have some typical symptoms: Active cold Passive cold can be described accordingly:

1. Hidden actions, for example, storing anger conveyed behind people's back or by subtle remarks, silent treatment or breathing, avoiding contact with the eye, putting down gossip, anonymous reports, poison pen letters, stolen and conning.

2. Manipulation that leads to violence and then patronizes forgiveness provokes hostility but remains on the sidelines, emotional blackmail, real tearfulness, feints disease, sabotages, sexual harassment, using a third party to transmit negative feelings, maintaining money or resources.

3. Auto-blame is overly critical, attracting criticism, such as apologizing too often.

Self-sacrifice, as too helpful, points out the best, quietly makes long signs of suffering but refuses assistance, or rejects gratitude, and makes friendly digs where it is not forthcoming.

4. Ineffective, such as committing yourself and others to failure, choosing to rely on unreliable people, being prone to accidents, underestimating sexual potentiality, and expressing frustration at meaningless things that are negligent.

5. Dispassionate, such as smiles, cooling, sitting on the fence and other people sorting out things, damping feelings of substance abuse (to include overeating), sleeping over, not reacting to other people's anger, refrigeration, indulgence in sexual practices that suppress spontaneity and turn participants ' objects in a state of excessive time for machines.

6. Obsessional activity, such as being tidy and safe, continuously testing, over-dieting or over-alimentation, requires the complete accomplishment of all work.

7. Evasiveness, for example, to turn your back on the crisis, to avoid conflict, not to fight, to become phobic.

Violent rage the violent anger signs are

1. Threats, such as threatening people, by telling how you could hurt them or their future, pointing your finger, shaking your fist, wearing offensive clothing, pulling up on the door, putting on a horn, slamming doors.

2. Hurtful, such as physical violence, verbal abuse, and cruel comments. Break trust, play loud music, use foul language, ignore the feeling of people, knowingly judge, accuse or punish those who have committed acts that they are not supposed to have done.

3. Destructive, such as harmful objects, which kill a relationship between the two, drive slowly, drink too much.

4. Bullying, such as persecuting, intimidating, pushing or firing, using intimidation to intimidate, screaming, using a powerful car that drives pedestrians out of the road, and battling the shortcomings of others.

4. Unfairly accuse others of their actions, blame them for their own emotions, make general allegations.

6. Manic, like speaking too quickly, walking too quickly, working too much, and expecting others to fit in, driving too fast, carefree.

7. Grandiose, such as demonstrating, voicing distrust, not delegating, being a poor loser, just trying to concentrate, not listening, talk about the heads of people, expecting kissing, and make-up to solve problems.

8. Egotisms, such as ignoring the needs of others, not listening to support requests, queue jumping, and driving' slicing.'

9. Revengeful, such as over-punishment, refusal to forgive and forget, and harmful memories from the past.

10. Unpredictable, such as blowing warm and cold, violent rages toward trivial grievances, indiscriminate attacks, retaliation for the good of the blue, damage for others obviously, the use of beverages and medications known to destabilize the mood and the use of illogical arguments.

Tips on control of Anger

1. Relaxation

Basic relaxation tools can contribute to the calming of angry feelings, such as deep breathing and relaxation. Some books and courses can teach you techniques of relaxation, and you can use them in every situation once you know these techniques. If you are in a partnership with both partners, it might be a good idea for you both to learn these techniques.

You should take some simple steps:

1. Breathe deeply, and you won't be reassured by breathing from your mouth. Picture the breath that comes from your "good."

2. Say a soothing word or sentence gradually like "relax," "take it easy," and say this to yourself while you breathe deeply.

3. Using imagery; imagine your memory or imagination as a calming experience.

4. Slow, non-strenuous yoga exercises can relax your muscles and calm you down a lot.

Practice these methods every day. Learn to use them when you are in a tense situation automatically.

2. Restructuring of Cognitive

. Put, this means changing how you think. Cognitive restructuring Irritable people tend to curse, swear, or speak in very colorful terms, reflecting their inner thoughts. If you're frustrated, your thought can become overly dramatic. Try to replace these theories with rational ones. For important, instead of saying to your yourself, "oh, it's terrifying, it's terrible, everything is ruined," say to yourself, "it's frustrating, I can understand that I upset, but this is not the end of the world and getting angry isn't going to fix it anyway." "This system never works," or "you still forget things" isn't just misleading, it is also meant to make you believe your frustration is justified and that the problem can never be solved. They also alienate and humiliate people who may be willing to work with you on a solution otherwise.

Note which getting angry will not fix anything that doesn't make you feel okay (and may make you feel worse).

Logic beats rage, as anger can quickly become unreasonable, even if it is justified. Using hard cold logic on your own. Note that the world "does not get you," you have some of the rough places in daily life. Do this whenever you're frustrated, and it will help you get a more positive attitude. Angry people tend to ask for things: fairness, appreciation, acceptance, willingness to do something. Everybody wants these things, and when we do not have them, we're all upset and frustrated, and unhappy people are demanding it, and their anger is becoming angry when their demand is not fulfilled. Angry people must become conscious of their unreasonable existence and turn their demands into desires as part of their cognitive rehabilitation. In other words, to say,' I like' is something better than to say,' I want' or' I need' something. You will experience usual reaction frustration, disappointment, hurt, but not anger when you are unable to get what you want. Many angry people use this rage to avoid pain, but the hurt doesn't go anywhere.

3. Problem Solving

Our anger and frustration are sometimes triggered by certain and inevitable matters in our lives. Not all anger is misplaced, and it is often a positive, natural response to these problems. There is also a cultural conviction, and it adds to our disappointment that this is not always the case. The best way to get to this point is not to focus on finding a solution, but instead on how you deal with the problem and how you tackle it.

Make a plan and monitor your progress. Resolve to give it your all, but don't blame yourself if the result isn't coming immediately. You are less likely to lose patience and to fall into all-or-nothing thought if you could approach this with the best intentions with efforts and try to face it front and front, even if the problem is not resolved right away.

4. Better communication

People with anger tend to make decisions and behave, and some of them may be very incorrect. If you are in a heated discussion, the first thing to do is calm down then think about your responses. Don't say the first thing that reaches your mind, but slow down and carefully think about what you want to say. At the same time, listen carefully to what the other person says and take your time to reply.

Hear what is at the root of the anger, too. For example, you like some freedom and personal space, and your "significant other" want more contact and proximity. Do not retaliate by painting your friend as a jailer if he or she starts complaining about your activities.

It's normal when you're attacked to be defensive, but don't fight back. Listen instead to the underlying words: the message that this person may feel neglected and unloved. You may need a lot of careful questioning, and you may need some room for breathing, but don't allow rage or the conversation of a partner to spin out of control. Holding your coolness will avoid a disastrous situation.

5. Using of Humor

"Silly humor" may lead to several ways to alleviate anger. First of all, it can help you get a more balanced view. If you get upset and call someone a name or say it in some creative term, pause and see what this word will look like literally, for instance, when you think of a coworker as a' dirtbag' or' single-cell life' you can imagine a large bag full of dirt (or an amoeba) at the desk of your colleague, talk on the phone, go to meetings. Do this whenever another person comes into your head. If you can, take a look at what the actual thing might look like. It takes much of the anger away, and laughter can always be trusted in a tense situation.

The fundamental message of highly angry people is, "Things go my way!" Angry people often feel that they have a moral right, that any blocking or change in their plans is an unsustainable indignity and that they should NOT suffer that way. Other people may do, but they don't!

When this urge is felt, he suggests that you imagine yourselves as a god or goddess, a supreme leader, who possesses streets and offices, walking by himself in all situations and taking your way, while others refer to you. The closer you get out of the invisible scenes, the further likely you are to realize you are perhaps unreasonable; you will also understand how insignificant things are about which your anger is real. There are two steps to use entertainment. First, don't just "laugh away," instead, use humor in helping you more proactively, face everyone. Second, I wouldn't give up cynical and harsh humor; that's just another form of unhealthy frustration.

What these techniques share is a refusal to take you too seriously. Anger is a dangerous emotion, but it often goes hand in hand with thoughts that can make you laugh when investigated.

6. Changing the Environment

It is sometimes our immediate environment that causes us frustration and anger. Problems and obligations that weigh up you and make you feel angry with the "hole" in which you seem to fall and all the people and things that make this pit.

Give a break to yourself. Make sure that you have a "personal time" that you know is particularly stressful. Another Instance is really the working mother with a lifelong rule: "For the first fifteen minutes, nobody will speak to Mother if the house is not on fire." After She feels so much better this small quiet time prepared to deal with children's demands without revealing them.

7. Some other suggestions to ease up your timing:

When you and your wife talk things during the night, you might be sleepy, or busy, or perhaps it's a habit to change the times when you chat about important things so that these discussions don't turn out to fight.

Invitation: If you're upset with your child's messy room every time you step through, shut the door. Don't take a look at what's bothering you. Don't tell, "Oh, my kid is supposed to clean up the room. I don't have to be mad!" The idea is to stay calm.

Alternatives: if your daily traffic path leaves you in frustration and rage, offer yourself another route, less congested and more scenic, a project-learned one. Or consider another option, like a bus or a shuttle train.

Managing Your Child's Anger

Wrath is the symbol of child frustration. If you do not allow the child to get rid of the cold syndrome and remove the root cause as well as the rage, your child might be in deep trouble in the future. Anger management in kids also calls for parents ' immediate attention.

Identification:

If children suffer from anger syndromes, they are quite easy to identify. Your child will be angry with the slightest difference from what he/she expects. S / he's going to show stubborn behavior. S / he appears to whine and scream unpleasantly when you contradict him/her on the simplest things. Some doubt about what he/she does and feels would make him / her display rage. The anger occurs almost when one wrong finger moves. Sometimes it will make it even worse for your child to take aggressive action. Wrath leading to violence is worse than wrath without abuse. There are other times when your child is silent. In other words, the child stays, but the anger doesn't come out. The negatives associated with cold will continue to accumulate in your child's unconscious mind and ultimately lead your child to a much deeper psychological problem. Anger, followed by silence, can be observed in circumstances where your child perceives it to be clearly negative and does not respond or react roughly to your interactions and other messages. Anger is, therefore, clearly identifiable in every shape. As we will see next, wrath syndromes have a significant negative effect on people.

The hazard of anger syndrome:

The child's anger syndrome is dangerous for both the child and the parents. There are short-term and long-term risks for both parties. The short-term vulnerability to your child primarily involves an unequaled everyday life. An example could be that your child angrily reacts to the suggestions of his / her teacher and may chat back. The immediate effect of this action is the negative feeling that the teacher is making of your child and maybe a lack of meaningful consideration to the child in the future. It might not be easy for your child to make friends with other children. Another example is that he/she will disturb a visitor visiting your house.

The long-term impact of prolonged wrath and abuse has been shown to be catastrophic. The child would grow up as an angry and demanding person, perhaps a bully. As a result, the rest of society never likes him/her. In some situations, it even contributes to the creation of a criminal mentality in the child, and the implications of such behavior are serious in nature. As an adult, your child's rage problem is not music to your ears. You may have to answer concerns about your child's actions in the short term. You may have issues with neighbors, visitors, and others for your child's rage. In the long run, you may not spend a happy age because your child is in the right section of society or is not seen in society with respect. You would be further hurt because your child could even stop bothering you. These are not ideal for any of you—yes, each of them poses a certain kind of threat.

Causes of anger syndrome:

Anger syndrome occurs most of the time, when your child's thinking is in the wrong state. In most situations, learning addresses the social interactions research phase in which your child has a role to play. The kid seems to interpret the truth differently than it is. The measurement error can be of various types. The child will feel that he/she should be young and not be responsible.

Any responsibility or transparency is heavily placed on him. The child also has a perception that angriness gives it power and control over you and that it can lead to a sense of victory. He could be explaining that you are not paying adequate attention to his needs and that getting angry will help him get the attention he deserves. The explanation for triggering rage syndrome is simply to try and imitate the child's offensive media. TV and the internet are often exampling of this kind of publicity.

The parent acts to alleviate rage in your child:

You must take the necessary steps to eradicate your child's anger syndrome. You must ensure that your child grows slowly but surely with a sense of responsibility and accountability for its actions. S / he starts virtually every action with a strong sense of responsibility. This will make the child fun to interact with and would also have the requisite publicity simply because of his accomplishments. This would instantly add the sense of power and control that you may want, but it would be something you have accomplished and know the value it holds. You want to make sure that, as a responsible parent, the child knows that he or she cares for every corner he or she wants. You should also be vigilant during your child's development so that he/she is not exposed to inappropriate media like hate transmitting outlets, abuse, and other things with a negative connotation.

After you have tested the condition so that your child likes to live, you can find that any frustration syndrome that your child has shown before slowly reduces and ultimately disappears. Your child will control temperament and moods perfectly and will be back on track in his / her life.

Chapter Two: Anger and Health

The health effects of rage are more related to length than frequency and intensity. The normal experience of open frustration only takes a few minutes. But there can be subtle types of frustration such as rage, impatience, irritability, grudge, etc. Consistent, persistent levels of rage make a person five times more likely to die before he's 50 years old. Anger raises blood pressure, increases the threat of stroke, heart disease, cancer, depression, anxiety, and, in general, depresses the immune system (scared people have a lot of aches and pain or get a lot of colds and stomach upset or flu bouts). To make matters worse, angry people appear, through other habits, such as drinking or smoking or compulsive behaviors, such as workaholism and perfectionism, to seek relief from stress caused by Anger.

Laboratory experiments have shown that even subtle types of frustration influence problem solving and general performance. Beyond elevated error rates, Anger diminishes and stiffens psychologically, leading to vague alternatives. The angry person has a "right way," which is always the best way to do things if picked in frustration. You can't do anything angry (resentful, irritable, shiny, irritated, chill) that is better than not angry.

Since it functions as amphetamine on the entire central nervous system, rage often causes a physiological "crash," which often happens as depression when the problems that cause the frustration remain unsolved. Think about it. Think about it. The last time you became really mad. Afterward, you were really sad. The more upset you are, the poorer you get. And that's just the physiological response, even if you're still doing something while you're angry, like hurting someone that you love.

What's the question of Anger?

A dangerous myth of a "risk issue" limits its scope to violence, assault, injury, or destruction of property. But this only describes one of a lot of Anger. You have a question of rage, if some kind of latent frustration –you may not even be aware of it–lets you do something that is not in your best interest or prevents you from doing your best. This may include anything small, like positioning a cool Wall in you or others persistent impatience or a low tolerance to irritation that impairs troubleshooting and efficiency.

Regardless of the form of rage, you are in danger of reacting with indifference, with your emotions, feelings, and actions completely controlled by anyone or anything you respond to. The more emotional you are, the more vulnerable you feel; basically, rage is a cry of impotence.

The three steps of self-compassion and consideration for others make us practically immune from the wretched consequences of wrath. The first step in self-compassion is to see the source, which is some sort of core wound (feel unimportant, disregarded, accused, deprecated, guilty, untrustworthy, rejected, weak, unlovable), as a symptom or defense (fear, coercion, Anger, odious behaviors). Secondly, the heart wound must be validated (as I now feel), and thirdly, it has to improve (this action or incident or failure or mistake doesn't imply I am unimportant, desirable, or lovable). It is compassion for others that acknowledges, validates, or embraces their symptoms, defenders, and gross actions through a core injury. Compassion does not justify disgust. This stops us from harming the already injured person, which helps us to focus on modifying unwanted behavior.

Control of anger management Regulation of Anger means repairing the hurt caused by internally restoring the central personal value that seems to be weakened by someone else's behavior. Anger management, by contrast, calls for a permanent injury that triggers the wrath but redirects its consequences to avoid violence and trouble. Regulation by indignation follows the concepts of emotional intelligence: awareness of inner experience, the ability to control the sense of one's emotional experience, and empathy for others ' emotional experiences. HEALSTM, an excellent management method, prevents the impotence of rage by supplying the feeling of inner strength, well-being, dignity, and consideration for others required for optimal health and solution. HEALSTM is a technology that automatically invokes a reaction of self-pity and compassion for others when rage and other defenses are triggered, concentrating instead of attacking the person on solutions to the problem. More than 90% effective at decreasing frustration at problem-solving and productive levels of performance, HEALSTM can be mastered in three or less training sessions.

Your Children's Anger: Who has power?

Since the very beginning, each parent has been painfully aware that children can do a lot to irritate, thwart, and otherwise turn their careers ' good feelings into hellish moods. The very same animals that look like little candy while they sleep can almost cause headaches, disturbing stomachs, jangled nerves, muscles exhausted, weak bones, and emotional and sensory circuits overloaded.

But there is one thing that children can't do even the most exuberant or obstinate: they can't make us mad. We can not compel us to give up our emotional experience internally. Consider the psychobiological role of rage to grasp this scientific fact that seemed to be flying in the face of common sense.

How Anger is a Problem in families If we feel threatened, indignation is the strongest of all emotional experiences. Anger exists to mobilize instinctual fighting or flight response that protects against predators; Only other emotion that triggers each group of body's muscle, including the organ. Our children aren't predators, of course. For the vast majority of marital issues, vengeance is overcrowding and underthinking. Using this fight or flight response at survival level to address daily family problems means using a rock to disable a lamp or tank to repair a computer.

Is anybody so stupid enough to turn off a rock lamp? Everyone is that dumb when mad. The problem is not about intelligence; it's about how hurt we are. Anger is always a hurt reaction. It can be physical pain, so you don't pray when you bang your thumb with a hammer while you are trying to hang a picture.

However, much more often, Anger is a response to psychological hurt or a threat of harm in the form of a reduced sense of self. Psychological hurt sensitivity depends entirely on how you feel about yourself. If your feeling of self is weak or unorganized, anything can make you angry or irritable. If it's strong and incorporated, life's threats and grievances just roll your back.

For example, if your day was a good one, if you feel guilty, you may be a little bit like a failure, or simply disregarded, devalued, or irritable, you may come home to find your child's shoes in the middle of the floor and respond with, "What lazy, greedy, unthinking, little brass!"

The difference in your reaction to the actions of the child lies entirely within you and depends entirely on how you feel. In the first example, the actions of the infant seem to diminish the sense of self: "If he was concerned for me, he won't; if my child didn't bother me, I shouldn't be worth caring for." In the second case, personal importance, interest, strength, and lovability are not diminished by the children's behavior. There is, therefore, no need for frustration. To solve the problem of the shoes in the middle of the floor, you do not need a tank. Rather, the question is how the kid is trained more carefully in his conduct; you will not humiliate him because you feel humiliated. His reaction to humiliation is the same as yours: an unwillingness to see the viewpoint of the other person, an irresistible desire to blame, and an urge to revenge or punishment.

Modeling Children's Anger Management Because their emotional maturity is considerably less advanced than their parents, for the same reasons as adults, children are angry, mostly to protect the sense of themselves from pain and temporary decrease. All children and adults feel bad about themselves at the moment of anger. It will only make things worse if angry people feel worse about themselves. Alternatively, children must learn from their parents that the sense of themselves is inner and can only be controlled within themselves. We must restore their sense of core value while respecting the rights of others, which means controlling the desire for retribution by validating the wounded and encouraging the impulse for vengeance and by recognizing the viewpoint of the victim to whom wrath is directed. You will only learn to do this by watching your parents.

Mastery of three stages of self-compassion and consideration for others renders us practically immune from ill effects of rage. The first step of self-compassion sees a cause that is a kind of heart injury (feeling unimportant, neglected, accused, devalued, guilty, untrustworthy, denied, impotent, unlovable) underneath its symptom or defense (anger, fear, coercion, degustation). In the second place, the core wound (this is how I feel right now) should be validated, and in the third place, modified (this action, occurrence, frustration, or fault doesn't mean I'm irrelevancy, indispensable or lovable.) Compassion for others is the acceptance, affirmation, and encouragement that a core wound triggers their signs, defenses, and disgraceful actions. Compassion does not justify disgust. This stops us from punishing the injured person, which helps us to concentrate on the unwanted behavior.

Wrath Regulation Some of the common rage activators we consider core hurts: feelings of neglect, unimportant, accused, guilty, distrustful, depreciated, ignored, helpless, caring. When triggered, core injuries include the sense of self in solving the problem that significantly distorts thought, blows the problem apart, and increases the emotional intensity of the answer. Clearly, the child is only responsible for the behavior, not your sense of self.

We need to reduce the sensitivity of these activators in order to regulate frustration. We must learn to see rage as a warning, not to blame our children for having fooled the activator, but to look inside ourselves to reset this triggered core hurt, that is, to restore core value, a sense of personal suitability and worth. With the sense of self that is no longer at stake, the question, no longer a cause of self-decrease, can be solved as it is: a call for greater attention/effort, dispute, deceit, or mistake.

Through three structured learning sessions with a regular practice between sessions, emotional control abilities can be taught very quickly. However, it is the self-regulation of the impulses of wrath and resentment, whether learned from training and past experience, which controls the activators of righteous anger internally, optimal work efficiency, personal happiness, successful parenting, physical and psychological health, and the ability to sustain sustainable attachment relationships.

Kids and Energy

I'm not sure why I'm getting a lot of questions and stories about children and energy, perhaps because it's spring. I would place all of them in this broad category, but we have addressed specific subcategories: children and ADHD, children and rage, children, and computers.

Children and ADHD

Let's begin with children and ADHD. In the USA, there seems to be a big trend to "monitor" our children's behavior in school. This method, I am NOT in favor of.

How is there such an ADHD epidemic in our children? I don't want to make it too convenient, but I think one explanation is that our children don't have the opportunity to run around and spend their time in previous generations.

Children have had to play in the parks, the streets, and their courtyards in the past. It is less and less common today. Families are too terrified to allow their children to be unattended, and rightly so! Some predators would hurt your kids. Nonetheless, however, children still need to spend their time.

Also, the things they have at home, including playing video games, watching TV, or using the home computer, and talking on mobile phones are sedentary. None of this gives you the chance to release steam unless your children are like my niece, who is peaceful when speaking on the phone.

Instead, we send them to school and wait for them to sit still. Furthermore, many schools minimize physical education for our children, and I have also recently found that certain schools' forbid children from playing in recess or using other playground equipment because they are afraid of a claim for physical injury. Is it any wonder that our children have trouble?

I know now that parents and teachers have children's stories that were tremendously helped by adding Adderall, Ritalin, Dexedrine, or Concerta to the daily diet. When you know a baby helped with its medicine, I'm not saying to quit it, but I believe there are at least three others who also exhibit all of the ADHD behavior that is designed to reduce the medication for each child that is being supported.

The physician knew whether the patient got the actual medicine or the placebo, it was actually better to have the placebo. Is it possible for some children to have a placebo effect?

If your child shows what you or the teachers think is unnecessary energy, do your best to create circumstances where that child can consume energy. I have two boys, and both could be diagnosed as children with ADHD. It was very physical. Thankfully I lived in the country during a time when parents simply sent their kids out to play. I also spent lots of time running around for different athletic events–YMCA football, soccer, flag football, basketball, you get the idea. Which certainly helps.

Kids and anger management

A woman was spoken with during the weekend whose son is ten years old and said that she has issues related to anger management. We didn't really get into his individual actions, but it prompted me to think about certain implicit differences between men and women.

I agree that boys and girls cope differently with their frustration from an early age. In general, girls have a better feeling to think about it, while boys have to focus on it physically.

So if you have children, you would like to teach them verbal skills, but with the young, you need to give them the opportunity to work their anger physically — perhaps with a punching bag, racketball, running, or martial arts. The list of opportunities is indeed endless, but don't expect your kids to "talk about," at least until they have the chance to release the anger in a secure physical way.

Children and computers

This week, a mother contacted me because her child had disobeyed her computer limits and had snapped over her limits.

The mother had a need to protect and nurture her child in this situation. She wants to be able to supervise her daughter's time loosely on the computer, so she can possibly prevent adults who are victimizing children by finding them on the Internet. He also wants to support the physical activity of her child so that he limits the use of her computer and promotes external physical activity. Is this mom wrong? Is it wrong? Not totally. Totally not.

On the other side, her daughter wants to be on the screen. There are all her friends, and I want to know why she is not. They have no limits as long as this girl does. This girl is very well done on the computer, and she can build her friends ' website. She also has a great need for freedom and doesn't like being limited, and the computer is fun for her. She gets a computer to fulfill her love &

belonging, power, freedom, and fun needs. Is she wrong? Is she wrong? Not totally. Totally not.

How is this resolved? I think that the way to solve this problem is for mom and daughter to sit down and talk about what they need and want in the situation. If the child can encourage her mother to have the skills and knowledge to defend herself from predators and consent each day to take part in other healthy activities, her mother will ease her computer time restriction.

In this case, and many others like, if there was no rule to break, the daughter could not fulfill her freedom need with the computer. Sometimes we create the very behavior with which we try to stop our rules. If a person is in great need of freedom, he will eventually break the rules, particularly those that he doesn't like or make sense.

Parenting is one of the hardest jobs you'll ever have to do, and there's a big risk. We all do our best and look forward to good results. Fortunately, children generally thrive, even when we have good intentions.

Essential Life Skills for Worry-Free, Confident, Happy Kids!

Full school days, homework, out-of-school... These days, families are more distracted than ever. Kids are packed with historical facts and details that they memorize for the next exam. So, where and when are the core emotional and spiritual skills that represent the child's wholeness and not the unilateral mind taught? Essential life skills that help children to be carefree, confident, and happy are often taught within the boundaries of a classroom, and even diligent parents do not always know where to start teaching the skills that make happy children easy to live. So what are these qualities, and how are our little ones taught?

Self Esteem is the first skill to be learned. Without that, children face challenges that are poorly equipped and are incapable of meeting their demands and expectations, not because of lack of capacity, but simply because of their lack of faith. Through teaching self-esteem (yes, it is an ability that can be taught easily), kids feel encouraged to live and invest in initiatives that they would otherwise fail. Kids with high self-esteem are always seeking and fulfilling their goals. We never give up. They never give up. We know it has nothing to do with them, and it's a learning process, even mistakes. As a parent, your first step in having your child display unconditional love and acceptance is to show high self-respect. This does not mean discipline is lost. It clearly means distinguishing actions with the self-worth of your child. Both things are very different. A kid is precious and lovable simply because it exists. Actions are taken to understand how to live and how to accomplish our life goals best. Such two aspects must be clearly defined and isolated, and your child will flourish with unconditional love.

Attention is the second skill to be mastered. Attention requires attention to detail and intuition. We plugin and clear our minds from endless past and future thinking. Carefulness allows children as well as adults to feel the true happiness of life without stress and fear at the moment.

Management of tension and wrath are two other skills that are important today. High-tech toys and gadgets are abundant, artificial worlds are abundant, and children spend less time playing in nature. The management processes are simple and need only be strengthened to become an integral part of daily life. Stress and anger control exercises include deep breath, anger or stress recognition, meditation, exercise, journaling, and slowly counting to calm down.

Children must also understand the strength of their thoughts and minds. More than 70,000 ideas move through the mind on average every day. And yet we will pay full attention only to some of these reflections. Nevertheless, these thoughts establish our experiences eventually, for our lives are created in the unconscious depths of the mind. They are the ones they focus on most. As children start to understand the law of attraction and the power of thought, they learn that they can create a future by using their minds. We've been dealing with families who feel like they are victims of incidents and circumstances in their lives for far too long. We are not victims. They are not criminals. When we mature spiritually and emotionally, we begin to feel that indeed it's for a reason and why the experience is actually soul-creation. Only with this understanding do we begin to take our proper place when creators of our destiny and start to live a life fully awakened by knowing that we produce all things in our lives consciously and unconsciously.

Another vital ability for children to be happy and trustworthy is to live by values. Nothing gives the self or others more pleasure. Values are the one thing a person can hold on all of his life that really makes life worth living. Good deeds are done for one's values; one's commitment is offered because one holds the pledge. The truth is told, honesty is upheld, kindness shows, love is expressed, and life is worth living. Anything as we followed our principles. Live by ideals seems to give life an inexplicable joy. Values give life to what a beautiful painting does for a picture. It gives meaning where none existed before. People gain great joy from living a life of values. Values are taught to your children through your living example, as well as simulations and discussions.

The next idea for children is safe lifestyles. Most groups fall into this capability in life. Healthy ways of living not only feed the body with good nutrition and exercise but also take care of thoughts and positive people who elevate us. Healthy ways of life are crucial points based on life. You should not be overlooked, or the basic framework of happy living will slowly be broken down. Children feel best in healthy environments, in psychologically fit people, and in the ability and incentive to speak in good health. All these skills are illustrated by illustration and explanation.

A balanced life is a basic opportunity for children to learn how to balance research, work, and play. And adults are struggling for this. The bodies are going to tell us intuitively whether something is out of kilter. We fall ill, and we feel sick, we seem confused, or we just feel' off.' Intuitively, we know when we are unbalanced and must take a conscious decision to resolve ourselves by taking time off and taking care of ourselves. Children can easily find harmony by focusing on it, for example, by playing video games or playing on the computer. Lead him if your child struggles in this area. Set boundaries and go outside and play TOGETHER. Teach the basic skills and also how to use them. Having a balanced life means keeping safe and always feeling good.

Financial prosperity for children is the last of our education system's fundamental life skills. Many schools do "train" financially, but financial learning is different. Financial education and prosperity is a skill which goes hand in hand with the best use of your mind-your life resource. We don't live in the age of industry, but now we live in the age of information. New skills are a must for this new environment to succeed. Children need to know how to use their creativity and their passions to create opportunities and services that previously did not exist and to give value to their community. Could kids learn that? We may, of course. This needs us to start teaching outside the box and see the plentiful opportunities.

The transition is starting now, as one of the leading pioneers of the self-development Movement has stated: "If children know these basic life skills, the world will be transformed in just one generation."

Tips for Dealing with Angry Children

I'm sure you can tackle the problems of every day and the complexities of coping with angry kids. When you come back home after a stressful day of constant stresses, it can be impossible to have enough brainpower and emotional stability to manage your angry children. There is certainly no bigger mistake than to throw away your bad moods. While I know that' stuff' sometimes rolls down hills,' things' are rising and burning on you in this situation.

Are you aware that your will would pass to your children? If you've ever been or have been on the verge of becoming that issue, it's time to explore some effective techniques for coping with angry children.

You will find ways to help your children learn to cope with their own problems and needs. You should work with angry children effectively. Although the burden your kids have on you may seem low, they can also be overwhelmed by their frustrations. Anger is often a common human reaction to worry, stress, or pressure.

Try three techniques to help you cope with angry children and to encourage your children to overcome their frustration so that life is more fun for all.

1. The guideline number one for the care of angry children is... Wait for it! Wait for it! Seize every day for a few moments of rest. Stay ready to enter a new world. Tip No. 1 is... Push you to dig this rest for yourself. (Parents have an appropriate plan for alternation, which provides the children with their needs during this time.) Then you will build a wall between work stress and the outside world during these few moments of rest each day or alternating days.

Snatch every day for about 15 minutes. There is no better way to deal with angry kids. A hot bath, use bubbles. Take a bath. Take a shower. Shower. Read four pages of the novel you wanted to continue with. Count the fur of your dog on your shoes. It doesn't really matter. With practice, you will learn that these 15 minutes will allow you to create an effective barrier between work and home peace. Adjust this guide to fill your idea in these 15 minutes. Check and rehearse techniques by which you can brake pressures from your family life at work.

Dealing with angry kids requires your brainpower and guided energy to work at the same time to achieve some success. Taking this time, your mind can fully relax and relieve your stress and concern. While teaching your kids that not all of their needs are emergencies, your kids will also start learning that Mom and Dad, Grandma and Grandpa, or whoever' needs' to rest and to rejoin after a day off the house or in other home circumstances.

You discipline your children more efficiently, can think more clearly, cope more easily with their stuttering, and have a more comfortable home when addressing angry children successfully. You can then pay more attention to your angry young people and start teaching them by example.

Are you conscious that your kids can understand through your body language that your life is not all right? Recall that part of their "naughty" behavior is either a manifestation of children that represent your feelings or a forecast of your willingness daily. It is full of surprises to deal with angry children.

I know you don't want to hear it, but angry parents produce angry kids. As you experience your performance in agitation and anger, you will learn how to manage your moods to ensure that you are successful.

When your pressures and attitude (everyone has these!) are properly handled, you will be able to uncover the time for your children to play and deal with their problems. You will do better to manage your efforts to deal with angry children, increase your efficiency in disciplining them, and encourage them in their efforts.

2. Another way not to raise your children is to show them the wrath control techniques you use. Many examples which can help young children are

1) deep breathing,

2) taking a walk or a walk,

3) talking to their parents,

4) reading quietly.

Children are also being pressured, frustrated, and angry. Their stressors are, of course, distinct. Be mindful that your stressors rely on your age. To order to deal successfully with angry children, you must meet your expectations with your children's age. The young people bring home school concerns, just as you bring tension out of college. Anything you have done to reduce your stress and reduce your frustration and anger should function in a modified form for your children.

Make sure you don't raise your voice and explain these techniques. There'll be rolling eyes; that's all right. This is possible. Instead of shouting at the dog to stop throwing bricks, you would quietly have to push the blocks away.

(It is essential to allow your child to express your angry feelings adequately before you can agree on any action move for dealing with angry children. Confirm that everyone is out of a way, that means no hitting, no throwing, no screaming, no naming, and no' whatever your kids do' when they are upset. Nod your head and just listen carefully while describing what disturbs you. Patiently give instructions on how to use words when sharing feelings. For example, if he puts his doll in the toilet, you may say, "So, Johnny made you angry?" Your child might say, "Yeah..." or "Duh!." It is not essential. You have a reply now. You connect. Therefore, your child now knows that you are listening and caring about her concerns. All this work is far more critical than a swept road, or broiler pan.

3. Finally, make sure that every day you and your young people get enough sleep. I know that in our noisy lives this is difficult. The more you and your kids relax, the more easily everyone can deal with the pressures and challenges of today. Having plenty of sleep means you are always healthy and able to cope with the many

challenges of life. Then spending quality time with your kids will be part of your solution to your angry kids.

You should look at activities with your kids to see how they think and feel about all their hectic events. Find places to strengthen the system for the entire family.

These few thoughts, when you raise your children to be healthy, well balanced, and friendly children, can come in very handy. Keep in mind that they learn, change, and will never be perfect. There are going to be mistaken.

In communicating successfully with angry children, you will do all you can to become a good parent and prepare your young people to become the best possible individuals. Take an idea at once, use patience, remain calm, and, when appropriate, be guided and encouraged.

Eighteen years of my own family and eighteen years of experience in helping families with troubled youth have led to such powerful and simple secrets that secrets are shocking.

Consider the age of your children and the ___ ___ ___ are under, in the same way that your ___ ___ potentially overwhelm you. Anger is a con___ reaction to stress and anger. This is also true for countless children. Life is full of obstacles, and parenthood is immense. It's the biggest challenge that we face.

Chapter Three: Teach Kids to Control Anger, Not Vent It

The child who gets frustrated with a puzzle or argues with a friend has to learn how to handle the internal energy building before it explodes. Before the explosion, children can slow things down in their minds, and you can encourage them as parents. A wrath management plan has multiple elements, and one crucial step is to encourage children to stop when their feelings urge them to move forward.

Anger will inspire children and adults to behave and do or do things they regret later on. However, many children have more emotions than they can easily manage. That y they need a heart quality outstanding that God ulls self-control. "A fool blows his wrath completely, but a wise man holds himself under control." Make sure to read this verse again before you go on. There is, after all, a lot of modern thought that encourages people to undo or unleash their anger to reclaim emotional control. This is not the teaching of the Bible. Alternatively, a heart management plan is established that celebrates divine qualities. Please don't think that means repressing or filling rage so that revenge comes out later. Self-control means simply to harness anger's strength in a way that is not detrimental. Children can learn this, but preparation and much of God's grace are required. It is best to use a stop strategy to slow things down instead of encouraging them to intensify and help your family gain greater control over frustration.

The size of a child's stop sign depends on the strength of the rage. Kids who are very depressed need a bigger stop sign to face the problem, but kids also need to learn how to deal with the little stresses of life. Stay often requires some task or leaves the situation. Sometimes it only requires a moment's pause and a deep breath. The child has to take time to recognize the development of frustration and wrath.

You can even use three separate stop signs for younger children to illustrate your point. The little one only takes a few deep breaths. Method one can also involve walking a little to help the stress settle. The greatest is a break from the situation, which focuses entirely on settling down, usually in another room or away from the situation.

It's good to intervene whether the child is upset or already really angry. This step is particularly crucial for the enraged boy. Rage is the rage that holds you under control no matter how well you mask it. The best way to tell children that they are angry is that they can't think rationally anymore and that their indignation dominates them. We lost control. They lost control.

The reaction to anger is always to avoid. "You're too upset to speak about it right now if a kid is agitated. Go spend some time alone, come back, and tell me calmly why you're mad, we will continue to talk about it." Kids with an issue of frustration don't want to leave. They want to push ahead, express their frustration, decide to get the things they want and manipulate the situation sometimes with their anger. Stops don't seem normal, and children who don't manage themselves easily enter cold episodes of different magnitudes.

Don't jump into the war with your baby, whatever you do. Children look for ways to get you into a fight when they're angry. Stop it. Remove it. It's not successful, and the problem also increases. Learn to stop and teach your children to do the same thing. You will see a better ability to interact with your children without the problems of frustration. If you choose to fight it physically, then the problem in the child is no longer a heart problem. It is now a question of conflict management between two upset people.

A successful anger management strategy aims to reduce the strength of a child's frustration, the frequency of episodes of rage, and the duration of the recovery period. When parents and children work on a plan of anger, children become more self-controlled. Here are several instructions for managing anger in a house. Make it a regular part of your routine, and you will see considerable progress.

1. Never argue with angry children. Take a break and continue the discussion later.

2. Identify the outrage signals that your child is about to lose control of. Show them early and stop the interaction. Once you move, don't wait for explosions.

3. Help children understand rage as a bad attitude, a grumble, a glare, or a harsh voice in its various disguises.

4. Debrief after settling the boy. Next time, explore how to handle the situation differently. Even use a better way of dealing with the case.

5. Teach constructive responses to children. You might get help, talk, or walk away. These ideas help children to have a plan for what to do, not just what to do.

6. If angry words or actions harm someone, people will apologize and seek forgiveness.

By doing this stuff, you will teach your kids this: "But now you must get rid of everything like this: wrath, anger, provocation, slander and filthy language in your lips." It takes a lot of effort to build emotional control, and often, the family is a laboratory for this development.

Recall that the child's anger is the problem of the child. Do not engage in conversation until the volume decreases. Regulation of wrath is a crucial learning trait for children, and the time is no better than now. The structured stop in response to hot emotions helps children regain control and retains children's attention on the issue.

Most adults do not know how to deal with their increased intensity and progress rather than retreat. The natural tendency to become more violent when upset, but the best solution is to reduce the intensity before going forward. Families who need such a mechanism will go much further to help their children cope with their frustration.

100 fun activity for Talking

Top 10 Outside Toys for Children Under 12

If you're a mom, you probably know that it can be a difficult time in summer. Children's parents under the age of twelve frequently struggle with bored children. Only so many things are possible for a child inside. This is why children need to spend the summer outdoors.

Playing outside in summer is enjoyable, but without a few outdoor summer toys, many of the children will quickly get bored. If you are the parent of a child under the age of 12, you have several options for buying outdoor toys. Below are a list and a short overview of the ten most common external toys for children under 12 years of age.

(1) Water and sand activities

Sand and water activities tables are tables that allow children to play almost at the same time in the sand or in the water. The majority of tables are divided into two sections. A great number of businesses manufacture water tables and sand, so you purchase a wide range of many table designs. Most water tables and sand for children aged three and over are planned.

(2) Outdoor water sprinklers

How many children with no access to the pool have stayed cool during the summer years have been outdoor water sprinklers? Outdoor sprinklers come in all sizes. Modern sprinkler systems could be purchased; however, the sprinklers can be used to make large plastic animals, beach balls, and another popular character. All outdoor water sprinklers need to be hooked up by a garden pad.

(3) Water Guns

Related to water sprinklers above, water guns are a fun way to keep children safe without a pool. Water pistols come in all shapes, sizes, and types. You can buy a water gun suits your hand or palm, or you can buy one that is so big that it is waist-sized. Large water weapons tend to have more energy when it comes to water flow. It means that the majority of large water arms are not safe for children under 5.

(4) Water Plays Slip

Slide Slip and slides are called water slides. For years now, they have been a common outdoor summer toy for children under the age of 12. Slippers and slides work best on the hill, but a child can have fun even on a flat surface by running water. Most slides and slides are sold for extra fun with a sprinkler or a small wading pool.

(5) Inflatable water slides

Up to recently, slip then slide water toys have been the water slides only built without the pool for home use. Today large water slide is sold online and across the country in department stores. Such slides can be inflated and up to 10 feet in the air. They have a small pool in the field. Because of its big size, most water slides are designed for children over four or five years of age.

(6) Sandboxes

Currently, sandboxes are located across the country in millions of backyards. When filled with sand, sandboxes give the whole family hours of fun. Sandboxes may come as large plastic animals in typical box sizes or: the most common plastic turtles and crabs for children under the age of five.

(7) Teeter Totters

Many parents and children mistakenly think teters are intended for the park only. The reality is that there are many teeter tins built for backyards of all dimensions. Big teeth can often be stuck into the ground and thus easily used by older children or adults. You can also buy tiny, compact teeter tokens tailored for children under the age of 10.

(8) Grill and Grill Accessories

One of the most common outdoor toys to hit the market is toy grills. A large number of companies produce these grills; therefore, most retail stores have a wide selection of different styles. The grills will come with speakers, plastic food, and other grill accessories in all different sizes. Such toy grills make kids feel like an adult while cooking right next to their parents.

(9) Children's Garden and wheelbarrow accessories

For several outdoor activities, a child's wheelbarrow may be used. Children can move their toys using a wheelbarrow or support their parents in the garden. Most wheelbarrows can be bought for extra fun with additional garden accessories. Children's wheelbarrows come in all shapes and sizes, and so kids of all ages can enjoy this great outdoor tool.

(10) Bubbles:

It has often been considered the fun outside of toys, but they have been even more enjoyable because of the additional bubble toys. In addition to traditional bubbles, bubble-making machines are now available. In just a few minutes, these devices can often create hundreds of bubbles. Machines can also be used to create huge bubbles. There is another bubble accessory, besides bubble machines, which could create shapes of unique bubble and many more.

These are the top ten outdoor toys that are most common for children under the age of twelve. The good news is that virtually all these toys are inexpensive and perfect for backyards of nearly any scale. Why allow your child to suffer during a boring summer when many fun outdoor toys are within your reach?

10 Tips for Kid-friendly Holiday Outings

1. Next, ask a friend. Before you go on a great holiday, get a recommendation from a relative, family member, or trustworthy authority. Consider the age suitability of all behaviors.

2. Confirm specifics of the case by calling forward. Definitions of operation vary year by year. Avoid specific hour surprises, overcrowding because of planned field trips, etc.

3. Bring a sandwich! Prepare a snack. It is not much fun when you end up hearing,' I'm hungry!' The snack area (if there is) teams up with screaming kids and their adult mates. Bring a favorite snack to avoid trouble and additional costs.

4. Divide and conquer the roles of adults in the party. One parent should bring snacks and hand sanitizer for the babies. Another person should arrange transport. One parent should bring a camera to capture the memory of the holiday, while the other checks the weather forecast accurately.

5. Fix your fears. Address your fears. If your company meets Santa Claus or some other costumed figures, explain the relevance to ready children psychologically before the trip. For example, adults may portray Santa as a nice man with a soft white beard, and he loves kids. Viewing photographs can also help to understand.

6. Prepare dinner beforehand. After a long day of fun, children are starving and exhausted. Their parents do the same. The night before or the morning of your adventure, have a dinner which can be heated later in the oven or in the microwave when the children go to PJs.

7. Take a car ride toy. Keep the kids amused. Consider books or games that could be related to your holiday.

8. Childproof. Scan the area of the event for any small items that might be a danger. While many places address this issue in their design, many children also bring home products, including smaller toys appropriate for elderly children.

9. Clean those hands. Heal those hands. Germs crawl throughout the holidays but do not let their spirits dampen. Take a bottle of sanitizer such as Purell at the end of the trip.

10. Talk to your children. Talk to your children. Take the time to talk about the experience, what the children enjoyed, and share their thinking. This is an opportunity to encourage children to interact with competent adults and share their desires.

This is the Best Activity for Toddlers!

What really is Geocaching?

Geocaching is a worldwide GPS game that began in 2000 and is fast becoming a HUGE hobby, particularly with kids of all ages. It's much like the old hobby "letter-boxing," but much better. It's basically liked a global hunt for treasure. Players use handheld GPS devices (every cheap GPS works) to hide and scan throughout the world to find small containers (caches).

You create an account, and then you can add your zip code or address, and you will see a map that shows you exactly where all Geocaches are in whatever location you are looking for. Then you load and find the coordinates it gives into your GPS unit. When you're searching a list, you can find small toys that kids and other small children enjoy, or it's just a logbook to log in.

Why is Geocaching for Toddlers such a great activity?

In addition to the fact that children enjoy small toys, which are found in most caches, it is hunting thrill. Children love searching for and finding something before mommy or daddy. You love exploring and seeing new places.

Nearly every cache is child-friendly. Many are put in parks and in leisure areas so that your baby can play before or after hunting.

Overall Geocaching is just an excellent way to be fun, to discover new places, to meet new friends and above all, to link up with your children!

Weather and Math Activity for Children

The bad weather doesn't have to be a frightening time for kids. In reality, a stormy night can become an enjoyable family activity that can be educational and fun for all your family members.

The light produced by a lightning bolt almost enters your eyes simultaneously. But as light travels faster than sound, you're still going to see it before you hear it. The light appears almost instantly at 186,000 miles / second as the sound hits you at about 770 miles/hour. It takes just 5 seconds to travel the distance of one mile at this pace. We can easily calculate how far the lightning is from here using this knowledge.

To continue this operation, find a safe place and watch for lightning flashes on the next stormy night. Once you see a strike, count the number of seconds between the flash and the thunder that follows, or use a stopwatch.

After you have identified the seconds between the initial strike and the thunder boom, you have to divide the seconds by 5 to approximate the distance. For example, if you see a bolt of lightning and hear thunder 9 seconds later, it's about 1.8 miles away. This figure was found by dividing nine by 5, equivalent to 1.8.

Here is another one: How far would a lightning strike be when the first lightning bolt takes 21 seconds to hear the thunder? Take 21 and divide it into 5, and your response should be 4.2. The lighting hit is, therefore, about 4.2 miles away.

You should realize that this approach is not always 100% effective. The thunder you hear might not necessarily match the lightning you see. Alternatively, it could all be from another lightning bolt. Not all lightning hits the floor, so many lightning strikes out of sight, even if you still hear the sound of the thunder.

Health will definitely be a top priority for lightning observation. You should stay away from metals, devices, and large objects like trees or light poles.

You don't have to be a skilled meteorologist to see how far lightning is away and enjoy watching the weather. All you need is a stopover and secure area to watch for lightning to become a fun and educational experience an otherwise unpleasant evening.

Simple and Fun Activities at Home for Kids

Parents today have several resources to help their children move forward in today's fast-moving society. Now more than ever, schools are facing a variety of problems: overcrowding Teacher Shortages Budget cuts

Support workers Toddler and Preschool: Knew that parents, nannies and nursing workers could provide children with enjoyable school activities regardless of their age? Children and pre-school children must learn the basics before entering kindergarten. Every pre-school child should know basic and unique skills. Simple instructions, activities, and communication are a few basic elements, but while these are essential skills, kindergarten teachers would like children entering school to have certain competencies such as the ability to read clear books, to write their names, and simple mathematics to name only a few.

Parents, nurses and daycare providers can now visit a variety of websites generally made up of teachers or retired educators to download and print activities for children that address the fun skills needed to enter kindergarten. It doesn't have to be 100% educational; a lot can be said to print out coloring pages for your kids. Coloring is an educational aspect of itself as children discover their environment through color, form, and everyday artifacts.

Children's kindergarten and Beyond Fun school activities do not always need to be on paper. Some of these fun activities are now available for children of school age. Many teachers use the Internet in various ways: computer skills development Interactive learning reading and math training activities continue to build their abilities. Each of these fields is then worked on during school until the children graduate from universities and start their careers.

Children learn by doing, and the more they are introduced to the skills they need to practice after graduating from a school or university, the better.

Internet access to websites that encourage education skills often offers fun at home for children who experience learning from their classroom to their homes so that the skills that are learned during school holidays or summer holidays have little or no change.

Though Internet access is essential, practices that help the skills taught should be matched with physical hands.

While coloring and performing activities on the paper or on the website are fun for kids, it is equally important that kids play enough time to run, jump, and be children.

Photography for Children

Photography is one of the most accessible forms of art, and children get a real start on camera equipment. Particularly fun for children these days because digital cameras let them see what they take immediate images of.

If you want to help your child discover the photography world, you can do so in several different ways, based on age and skill level. This is what you need to know to get started.

The first thing you have to consider is your children's digital camera. Very small children can use robust' drop-proof ' cameras in toy shops or online. Although these cameras take photos of relatively low quality, your child will still get used to taking images, and you will avoid the nervousness associated with providing a child with an expensive piece of equipment.

You can pick up a high-quality digital camera for children below $100 or spend a little more to get a camera that lasts a little longer. You can also give your child your old camera when you decide to upgrade.

Before you purchase a camera from your child, be sure to read the camera reviews to make sure it meets your needs. You will find the right camera by doing your due diligence in advance. Many digital cameras have many choices, but your child will probably not need more than the focusing options and some other settings. Don't give them more than they can, or it's too stressful.

If your child has a camera, you will allow them to use their camera in various projects and fun activities. The first step is to take your camera wherever you can. Walking in the park, visiting the grandmother's house, and even a simple supermarket trip could be a photo adventure for young children. The fact that their camera is ready to use allows them to take more pictures.

Help them evaluate their photography and work at framing shots if your children are in the older elementary grades. Digital cameras can really help in this because every shot your child will provide immediate feedback. When they get used to their camera, they learn basic principles of photography, such as third-party law and backlighting techniques.

The digital cameras can really concentrate on playing and shooting because you don't have to think about wasting movies. Your children can only shoot and keep the pictures they are most proud of.

Encourage your children to take more images using a variety of techniques and viewpoints. Encourage them to press the various buttons on the camera to see what they like best for different effects.

Ask them to record a day or a special occasion in a way they may not have imagined before. Perhaps at the dinner table, they will close down the dog's toenails or their water glass. Once the photographs are printed, encourage the children to write imaginative names, journal entries, or fictional stories that go along with their visual arts. You should challenge your child to complete photographic projects when you have mastered the basics. For example, your children can get photos of everyone in their family who makes silly faces. Throughout your day, you will take several pictures of your family pet or send photos of your favorite times to your grandparents.

See photos taken by others, whether in a magazine, a coffee table book, a website, or in a photo art gallery. Ask them about what appeals to each of their favorite photos. Which type of lighting, design, or special effects contributes to a photograph's mood?

In learning more about it yourself, you will join your child in his photographic activities. Take a course on digital photography or buy a book to share tips. You will improve the quality of your images and have a hobby that you two can share over the coming years.

Bowling Is A Great Activity for Kids

I think Bowling is the perfect children's sport. Most children can do this even if they face some physical challenges.

When they were very young, all three of her children started bowling. When he was six years old, her oldest child began. Her middle child and her youngest child both started at the age of five.

When a woman signed up for Bowling with her oldest child, she did this because he wanted her to have a fun activity with children of her age. He already tried to play baseball and did not like it; the boy scouts did not like him either. Bowling was the only other sport in our area available. And as her son was very shy, she decided to get him out in a fun social setting with other people. Bowling proved to be a good way. It was fair, and Bowling was done only once a week, so she figured her son didn't find it boring.

He enjoyed golf, and he loved Bowling. He started bowling on the streets with "bumpers." Bumpers stopped the bowling ball from hitting the gutter so that each child could at least knock down a few pins. This stopped the children from being depressed and abandoned. At the same time, the children had coaches who showed them how to bowl correctly. "Bowler of the month" awards every month were given to a child in each league. A child will work hard to improve and inspire his peers to be a bowler of the month.

There were celebrations for Halloween and Christmas as well as prizes. In addition, every time each child has a milestone in a bowling game (such as his first 100, 125, 150, or 200 series), the child has received a patch. The woman spent many hours sewing her children's bowling tops. Cutting on these patches was definitely a work of love because she hates to sew! Then bowling trophies (or dust collectors that her husband wants to call them) were awarded at the end of each year.

Her three children competed until they finished high school. In addition to Bowling, they learned a lot about commitment, teamwork, perseverance, coping with deceit, and how to cope with success graciously. Each one was given college grants from tournaments in which they participated and/or bowling clubs in which they were involved. And there were monetary incentives for them all too.

Your kids still enjoy Bowling. Both of her sons are a fun social activity out of college and bowl. Her daughter is in college and is a member of the bowling team of her college. She still enjoys competitive Bowling.

Bowling is a great life sport, I think. In comparison to sports like football, which are only available for short periods, Bowling can be enjoyed for a long time. For starters, there are senior citizens ' associations of people in their 70s, and in even their 80s, there are bowling every week in their local bowling alley.

Healthy loss of weight for children and adolescents

We love and want our kids to be safe. In reality, as we continuously surround the unhealthy, it is not always easy to introduce or maintain healthy food habits in our busy life. Western society currently contains many television programs with plenty of unhealthy foods, little exercise, insatiable fast-food restaurants, and not enough healthy food from the family at the dinner table.

The good news is, however, that there are many ways to help your kid or teen feel great about himself and shed those extra excess pounds without rapid weight loss schemes.

Weight loss begins in mind, and the way we see ourselves goes hand and hand. Together with unhealthy eating habits, at this tender age, a lot of children and teenagers are obese, not pretty, and many even find themselves fat. These unhealthy projections create energy for what is self-fulfilling. As loving parents, we can help our children by teaching them and sometimes even re-education. Before touching on the subject of food, however, it is necessary to understand and use the power of words and thoughts clearly.

Next, teach your child about imagination. Visualization holds a picture of the desired result. When a child understands that the mind is the creator of reality, it can start concentrating attention on what one desires instead of what one believes to be true or unavoidable. Let's say, for example, each day, you look in the mirror and think,' look how fat I am.' What happens over time will eventually manifest through your daily imagination and the influence of your own words and thoughts. The scale will gradually fade up. It will only confirm what you thought you saw in the mirror for you. Now the scale also says it, so it needs to be true. Do you see the endless cycle here? It is self-created and self-driven. This doesn't mean that food choices don't matter. But there are usually traveling partners who feel obese and get followed by healthy food choices.

Use the visualization power for good. Use it to make your perfect kid or teenage body the same. Sometimes it can be hard for a kid to picture how smaller she feels. If so, ask her just to imagine whether she is a little thinner or healthier and to see whether that is more beneficial. Tell her how she's going to feel when it's easy to go up and down or do anything that actually seems to be complicated because of extra weight. Close your eyes and involve your child in an imaginative daydream every day. It's a fun company. This brings you closer and allows your child to feel your support and love.

Even if you don't see your child or adolescent, ask them to imagine their target every day many times a day and make it as real as possible. Tell her to experience walking, playing, and moving within her new ideal body and constantly imagine how slender and healthy she is as she reaches its target.

Sadly, children who are overweight are often victims of bullying. Overweight children and those considered obese are actually much more bullied than other children. Your child will probably have experienced at some stage the consequences of bullying. This is a great concern for parents, and we want to assist our children to be happy, protected, and not victims. Your child may be humiliated by any bullying, but it is important that you discuss the issue openly. If you are unwilling to talk about weight loss, direct the chat so that your child can share his or her thoughts and feelings freely. Most kids come to us to inquire about answers. You know a change is needed; you just don't know how to start. Note that weight loss is a normal, simple product of healthy eating and lifestyle choices. The loss of weight should not be the only or main target. When weight loss is the only objective, a new, improved lifestyle may not last as old patterns may reappear after the weight has gone, and weight will most probably be regained. They want to make lasting change for the better, instead of simply reducing the effects of extra pounds temporarily, to the fundamentals.

Relaxation and regular visualizations should be combined to enhance the inner experience and bring it closer to home. Relaxation allows us to focus our attention completely and easily on the images. This can be achieved by returning the mind and body to a guided CD or by visualizing it.

Affirmations are another excellent way of teaching and helping children and adolescents while losing weight and being safer. "I make healthy food choices" and "I'm beautiful," and "I get healthier each day." "I'm peaceful with my corps" and "I love moving my body and playing" are all excellent statements. Affirmations in nature, are always positive and truthful. If a little boy doesn't feel beautiful, let him say, "I start to feel lovelier every day." Confirmations can preferably be used many times a day, and it's very encouraging to repeat in the mirror.

First, you must weed out unhealthy habits like eating comfort. Many unnecessary problems arise from "comfort eating." Physiologically, we know that certain foods have specific effects on the body— for example, chocolate soothes nerves and raises brain endorphins—

thereby decreasing body tension, allowing us to feel more content. When endorphins fall later, we hit more. It is important that your child knows the difference between genuine physical hunger and comfort. It is, therefore, essential to address every emotional problem and tension in your child's lives and to use stress management and relaxation techniques with your children.

Children sometimes learn from our own coping and sometimes learn these things by themselves. When you feel that your child can eat to comfort yourself, take additional time to speak and let your child know that you are there and ready to speak whenever you need it. Help your child experience the joy and relief of sharing genuinely with someone who cares about it. Teach relaxation techniques together with stress management to help your child grow and not receive comfort or stress relief for food.

Ultimately, be the healthiest family and help your child make healthy choices. Make sure that you understand these healthy choices and that you are proud of your kids. Make yourself an example by eating healthy, tasty foods that are good for you, at home, in the shop, and at home. Let your diet turn around organic fruit and vegetables and use them as condiments for everything else. If your kid or teen has something in particular, just don't buy it. It's harder to get if it's not in the building. Take some good library cookbooks and learn how to eat together and enjoy this new adventure.

Most importantly, note that good food should be friendly to be sustainable. When your family retrains its palate to natural foods, infuse the process with love and joy. Have fun making educated choices. Tell your child to feel the energy provided by better foods and the amount of energy available to the body. Healthy food affects the child not only physically, but also emotionally and mentally. In a few weeks, you will begin to notice dramatic positive changes. As parents, we will feel that our role in nutrition education ends when healthy choices become the common choice and less healthy choices.

Angry children need parents who understand two laws of commitment.

The ability of a child to manage and communicate emotions well is one of the key indicators of maturity. Most parents are frustrated with their children's emotional explosions and don't know how to respond without being involved emotionally.

Emotions are not bad, but the reactions from these emotions can sometimes be hurtful. Empathizing with the feelings can be a challenge for any parent without accepting the actions. Here are some tips for emotional sensitivity in babies.

First of all, children need to learn that their enhanced emotional feeling is a blessing and needs to be developed rather than seen as a flame to be accepted. An emotionally sensitive person has the ability to take clues faster than others in the environment. It's this kid who can normally go into a room before others can see it's wrong. God gave those who ultimately will be ministers, lawyers, or salespeople who know the best way to conclude an arrangement an extra heap of emotions.

There is, however, a distinction between emotional sensitivity and emotional response. Children can learn that frustration is good to recognize but not good to solve problems. After all, Jesus was furious, but he knew how to make productive use of this anger. "He looked upon them with rage, and he said to the man,' Layout your hand,' profoundly saddened at their stubborn heart. He took it out, and his hand was completely restored." Jesus did not respond to his frustration. He turned it around instead and did something positive. Children can be like Jesus like this, but some preparation is required. Unfortunately, many children simply respond to emotion, leading to negative words and actions. There's a better way, and the place to learn is fantastic.

Many children need to gain greater awareness of their emotions. Most children do not know they are upset until something has broken, or some harsh words have been screamed. You must see the frustration come before the reaction to be most successful. Another way to help children understand their feelings is to look at other people's emotions. One dad wanted to honor his 7-year-old daughter, Diane, who looked oblivious of her and others ' emotions. He used a diary and, at night, asked Diane to find examples of a friend or relative who was unhappy, happy, or stupid that day. He then asked: "How could you helpfully answer that person?" Each evening they continued this exercise for two weeks. After some time, it helped Diane get away from herself, look at other people's needs and feelings, and discuss ways to respond appropriately. If your brother is nuts, maybe it would be better to leave him alone or just ask a helpful question. She could offer help to her sad friend and then listen to empathically. When Mom is content, Diane will join the happiness by listening to and enjoying the story.

It is also essential to know how to express emotions. Some children are internal processors that churn away, but don't let others see their fight easily. Others are external processors that show to anyone who listens to what they think. Kids benefit from learning more about emotions and different kinds of feelings. Whether you are ashamed, sad, scared, or upset, children often react with anger and fail to acknowledge other emotions. Parents also teach important things by expressing their emotions. "It's like you're sorry you can't go to the game. I wouldn't be sad too if it rained out. But that doesn't mean that you can treat others together." Often, kids don't even know that they're upset before they hurt someone or do anything wrong. Maybe you want to help kids understand their feelings beforehand. For instance, the child who does not like instruction or constraint may reveal anger publicly, often with little or no vengeance.

One mom said, "When my 13-year-old son has bad behavior, he gets blunt in his actions and words. Mom has a raw tale to tell,' I'm not pleased with you.'" By making comments early on, Mom was able to raise her son's sensitivity before the incident took place.

When faced with the anger of a boy, it is essential to remember two rules of engagement. Second, don't be afraid of the feelings of your child. Kids sometimes use explosions as a way of protecting themselves to discourage parents from confronting them. See the emotion show as a smokescreen and look past it at the heart of the problem.

You may not choose to tackle emotional hotness, but don't let rage of your child deter you from fixing it. Too often, parents view the emotion as a personal attack and respond to it, losing any real advantage from the interaction. That's what makes us...

Commitment rule #2: Do not use your anger to overcome the anger of your child. A say said, "A compassionate answer turns away anger." Take a break when you start losing it. Come back later, working on it some more: "I was thinking about how you responded to me earlier when I asked you to do your homework. I want to make a point that may be helpful to you, and it seems that you think you should be able to wait and do your homework just before bed or in the morning before you go to school. Be mindful that children will leave thinking about what you said, even if their initial answer sounds like they didn't hear you. Prepare and pick the timing carefully without getting stuck in the emotional environment of the moment and help your child learn to handle the emotions more properly.

Chapter Four: Emotionally Abused Kids

No doubt, abuse is an emotional term. The emotional abuse issue is that it is not noticeable-it can't be seen anyway. Emotional abuse does not occur as it is seen in physical abuse cases in the form of bruises or broken limbs.

Emotional abuse is subtle and certainly more complicated than physical abuse to detect. The data doesn't come at you in the way physical abuse can happen. But, there's no question it's very real and extremely damaging for many children...

You just need to worry about how many incidents of physical abuse the police are overlooking. I see children with broken limbs that doctors, teachers, or social workers don't know... It's so difficult to believe, but it happens several times.

Abusers are devious and very creative in hiding the evidence from those in authority–and they seem to be deceptive and pretending that they are easy to manipulate. The thought of physically abusing the child could be so abominable for most people that it is too easy for them to fall for the lies of those who perpetrate such suffering on an infant. After all, parents should unconditionally love their children, do not hurt them without justification.

There can be emotional abuse in many ways. It could be a kid that does not get enough attention. Or it could be a girl who can grow up without restrictions and constraints on her behavior. Most children have access beyond their emotional maturity to abuse or events. They don't have adequate adult guidance. So many children receive only coldness and lack of affection instead of the comfort and the love they so desperately need. There are probably several examples where children lack what they need to grow socially confident and emotionally balanced.

Another example, a recent case of a combination of lack of limits and limitations on children's behavior, lack of proper guidance for adults, and complete indulgence of material possessions, is a very common problem.

But there's a terrible addiction to the emotional abuse list of this child. He's kept his mother's baby. He can not grow up and go through normal stages of development so that he matures as a normal child. He just can't be a normal little boy. He is actively encouraged to try something remotely adventurous if he hurts himself. His totally terrible behavior, one of the consequences of his lack of adequate motivation to develop normally. A baby with aggressive tantrums at its worst!

One big problem with this type of violence is that it is still concealed-his appalling behavior was, at first, the only true evidence with this boy. Often there are doubts, but there is no clear evidence to support these thoughts. Nonetheless, a lot of evidence has been exposed in this case! And everything is straight from the head of the horse-right from his mother's mouth!

One example of his immatureness was his anxiety and fear when we took the class on a hillside walk. The boy (he is almost nine years old) began to cry on the track, saying that he was afraid of heights. But we were on the road on the field!

On the playground, he was too afraid to walk on a wooden step, not more than eight inches from the ground.

He doesn't know how to play independently or with others. He doesn't take up social questions and thus annoys other children who don't always react to his lamentable attempts to play with sympathy.

This poor little girl-it was pathetic but sad... All of these examples raised my suspicions, and so I talked with his mother, who confirmed my thoughts. She said she actively discouraged him from doing boyish work. The nicest way she could be told she had to change and encourage him to grow up and act like an ordinary little boy. It could not happen during the night, but a beginning had to be made.

This is where building a strong relationship with parents is so vital that any sensitive issues can be tackled as quickly as possible.

But how sensitive I still had to discover this one! It's getting worse...

A few other children came to the class after I spoke to his mother, and they said that this boy was seen sucking a dummy baby...! Hard to believe, but a kid who is almost nine years old is still allowed to suck a dummy, or even encouraged... How sad, how sad... What a totally unacceptable treatment for a child... It's emotionally and utterly abusive! Completely cruel...

What happened? What happened? Well, his mother had to be contacted again and asked whether he could still suck a dummy like a baby!

Was it true? Was it true? Sadly, yes, it was true. His mom said he loved a dummy and wouldn't give it up!

In such situations, the strong relationship with parents pays off... Then you can take a very honest approach... You have to speak quite straight sometimes, but you can put on a dose of humor and understanding to make the process easier. Without offending people, there are ways to get your point across...

The mother of this boy was told how detrimental it is that a child can act in such a way that it is not compatible with his peers. He said the dummy would be put in the bin! A good result! A good result!

Will the dummy get rid of? All credit to her, sure, the same day it was binned. However, she was shocked that he was prepared to throw it away, a certain signal that he was ready to grow up. Even if she had done what had been told, she should not, first of all, have allowed this situation to arise and should have been guiding long ago to avoid "baby" behavior. Allowing her child to behave like a baby allowed other children to bully him and cause more emotional abuse.

By condoning bullying, children recognize their wrongdoing and make fun of it and cause other children needless agony.

Kids shouldn't bully other people, but you're almost encouraging a child to be so out of kilter with social norms... It's tough but real! Growing up is hard enough without adding unnecessarily to children's problems.

This boy-and his mother-is still a long way away, but his conduct is beginning to change. As a result, he will end up being much happier. It is difficult for him, but it's with any kid who must dramatically change their behavior to develop it properly to fit into society...

No doubt, abuse is an emotional term.

If Emotional Abuse may be a Child Abuse Form, Then Parental Alienation is Child Abuse

Experts from mental health agree that trying to break a child's relationship with a parent is emotionally abusive. If you are denied visits and unjustified access to your children, you will live with Dr. Richard A. Gardner's invented forms of child abuse. In this scenario, a parent manipulates the child to turn to the other parent. Therefore, if separating a bond is emotionally abusive, parental alienation is child abuse and needs to be recognized to counter it effectively.

The Federal Child Abuse Prevention and Treatment Act, at least, describe child abuse and neglect as any recent act or inaction by a parent or caretaker that outcomes of death, serious bodily injury or sexual abuse, or exploitation, or inaction, or an act that poses the impending risk of significant harm.

In terms of the relationship between the child and the alienating parent, a further description of the act of abuse is to be employed as a repeated pattern of the actions of the parent or of serious incidents that convey to them that they are useless, faulty, unloved, unwanted, harmful, or important to the needs of others.

In parental alienation, many behaviors are emotional, mental, physical, and spiritual abuses of children who are exposed to the parent who wants to oppose the other parent.

Amy J.L. Baker, who has over 18 years of experience in parent-child relationships and a health list for children, has seven measurable and harmful methods in parent alienation. They are verbal assault, isolation, corruption, refusal, terrorization, ignorance, and pressure. These tactics are used to convince children to meet the wishes of the alienating parent.

The dominant desire of the parent is to harm the target by making the children reject it, and by rejecting the target parent, they are showing their absolute loyalty to it. If their wishes are not fulfilled, the alienating parent feels disrespectful and often increases the intensity of alienation.

By rejecting the engagement of the target parent with their children, the alienating parent disregards the need of the children for their lives to be threatened and the emotional pain causing them not to receive their affection. Giving and receiving love between the parent and the child is essential to the development and maintenance of a healthy relationship between parent and child and the development of self-esteem of the child.

Once, for instance, Vincent separated from his wife, Lynn was accused of adultery and his incapacity to settle the dispute; he determined that it was best to leave their children, Elisabeth and Kate, with their mothers so that their lives and the violence causing them could not be disrupted.

The suspicions of Lynn arose from a comment by Andrea, a colleague of his, that she heard how attractive he is. While there is no evidence to support her argument, the assertion is equated with proof of an affair. She accepts it as true as she thinks of the distorted view. It causes her grief, and she promises to pay for hurting her.

After moving out, Vincent went on a daily basis and spent time with his daughters and used to call them to sleep to tell them that he loves them and wish them a good night.

Lynn was jealous of Elisabeth, Kate, and her father's relationship when she saw each other's affection. Cultivating rancor, she streamlined her sense that her participation in their lives is an effort to win them over and turning them against her to make custody easier for her. She is afraid to lose her identity as a parent under the surface if she loses custody.

Lynn constantly moved her dad in front of Elisabeth and Kate because of his insecurities and repeatedly said their dad moved out because he didn't want to be with you or love you. He thinks only about himself and only comes around to look good to his family and friends. She would follow up, "If he really cared for you and loved you, he would not have abandoned you." Believing that Vincent deserves punishment because of his faithlessness, Lynn even refused access to her children for cheating her.

This made Vincent angry, making him argumentative and demanding that Lynn respect his parental rights and not deny him the right and right to be part of his children. Lynn's resolve to keep the girls away from him strengthened with every progressive argument.

Because Vincent insisted on having access to his daughter, Lynn obtained an order of restraint from the court, forcing him legally to stay away or face time for disdain from the court. Elisabeth and Kate were essentially separated from their father. The lack of access to his children stopped Vincent from addressing misunderstandings about the breakup and how he felt about it and why he moved.

Successfully isolating the girls from their father, Lynn influenced them also to distance itself emotionally from him by repeatedly saying that he left them because he doesn't care for or love you, leaves the restricting order conveniently for his absenteeism. The underlying message is that because of his denial, and he is not deserving of their affection. Besides hurting Vincent, Lynn also misused her children emotionally to cover up her jealousy of the care they received and the fear that she would lose their custody and never see them again.

The psychologically and emotionally painful tactics of parental alienation are for children to deal with. Being loved, valued, desired, and cared for. This affects your self-esteem because often you feel the absence of the parent is your fault.

The thought that the alienating parent hates the parts that imitate the target parent may hurt them. They feel that they have any affection for the target parent to receive love and to have value for the alienating parent and must deny that parent. They fear that they will be treated as a traitor and maltreated like the target parent if they do not meet the emotional needs of an alienating parent.

Accepting these views may also lead them to believe that the love-affection of a parent is denied something is wrong with them. A parent's rejection damages them and diminishes their belief that others are forgiven for causing emotional tragedy as they grow.

Under the pretext of shielding her husband, Lynn makes Elisabeth and Kate unnecessary, dissolving their ties with her father to punish him for cheating her.

Parental alienation is child abuse because it breaks down safe walls between parents and children, causing children to know who they are and not. The limits are essential to children's self-esteem. They are the basis for protecting yourself, empowering you and being free to choose, and encouraging you to take responsibility and ownership of your life as you grow up.

Last note: It should be done in conjunction with a trained mental health professional to help children with parental alienation and avoid strategies so that they can understand why the parent who is alienated wants to separate the relationship they have with the other parent.

A counselor familiar with parental alienation, high-struggle custody disputes, and court proceedings is critical. This will greatly improve court hearings, and rehabilitation and a counseling aspect should be addressed to see which forms of violence are used. Once a decision has been made, a treatment plan can be inferred so that healing can begin.

Understanding Why Children Stutter When Speaking

What is Stuttering? (Also known as stuttering):

Stuttering is a speech impediment that often results in too many speech delays. For starters, I'm sure you've heard people who use a lot of' uh's, um's, and OH's' when they chat. These are known as inconsistencies (specifically interjections) in speech production and are quite normal–even for people who are not considered to have a speech production disorder. The problem is that there are too many inconsistencies that prevent a person from communicating effectively.

Stuttering is typically appeared during infancy and often persists for a lifetime. Parents are usually unaware of problems with speech development before their children start communicating in more than just a few words at a time. Stuttering often pervades several activities in a person's life, whether it is on the phone, in front of large groups, or perhaps in an environment which causes some degree of discomfort or stress in a person. In certain situations, the overall problem is that they struggle with home, education, work, and/or social contact.

As a result, many of these individuals would restrict their participation in basic activities to prevent contact with others. Why? Why? You are often ashamed or fearful of the reactions of others you try to communicate with. Many people can try to hide their language difficulties by halting in a sentence and pretending to have lost their thinking; others can put the word back in a sentence to get the words out, perhaps in an odd sequence, while others will not speak at all. In any case, it is really a shame for those who have broken off from others to remove the need for contact.

Here are some figures that follow stuttering: -

Stuttering mostly takes place between the years 2-1/2 and four years old. Although rare, primary school stuttering can develop.

Stuttering is most common in men than in women, and in fact, the risk of stuttering is estimated to be three to four times higher in men.

About 75% of pre-school students who can develop a stutter also stop.

Symptoms of stuttering:

As mentioned below, stuttering or stuttering is a speech disorder that often makes it difficult for others to follow the pattern of speech and information conveyed. Yet stuttering is more than one could imagine. Stuttered speech often includes an increased repeat of phrases, such as when a person might say, "I want a c-c cookie," or in speech sound extensions, such as in a c-c-cookie example.

Eventually, you can see part-word variations that would be like "What time is it?" individuals who seem to be out of stressed air and incredibly nervous while trying to communicate with others. There are many explanations, and knowing them will allow us to be more caring about the victim. Indeed, some stutterers seem to be getting the words "stuck" in their languages without a sound. Many stutterers describe this as words blocked in their throats. You know "what" you want to say, it's not going to come out without any pause in your language pattern.

An interjection can often be used to' produce' the sound(s) that the person tries to create and is often in the form of an' um," like' or another word or sound used to let the speech flow freely. Finally, everybody is trying to get the words out, but stutterers find it hard every now and then.

Stutter diagnosis: Not always all signs and symptoms of a stutter are to be found. Repeating phrases, voice prolongations, and interjections are easily observed by listeners who try to get the words out, but they also have trouble. The best course of action is, therefore, to consult with a certified speech-language pathologist (SLP).

The SLP identifies the number and type of speech disorders/disfluencies individual product within and in various situations during the evaluation:

How the person reacts to and handles the discrepancies made.

Frequency of speech.

Skills in English.

The severity of the symptoms identified and how their daily lives are affected.

Information will also be gathered on specific circumstances or factors that could lead to or lead to worse stuttering like teasing, mocking, or possibly fatigue, etc. The SLP will also need a history of changes, including the age at which symptoms have been first discovered, the patient's current age, and information on families who may also have stuttering.

After the assessment, examination, and interpretation of all facts, the SLP will be able to determine if a complex condition occurs and how it affects people's ability to interact and engage in their day-to-day activities.

Although the diagnosis among adults and children is quite consistent, additional factors are taken into consideration when diagnosing young children. The SLP will first and foremost determine whether it is likely to continue stuttering throughout the child's life, or whether it will potentially subside with time. The assessment will include numerous assessments, observations, and interviews to evaluate the likelihood of persistent stuttering.

The additional tests will include -Family history-a parent, grandmother, or mother of the child suffered from childhood stuttering, adults, etc.

Timeline-when the stuttering has started and how long it has been until now; 1–3 months; 4 –6 months; 6 months or longer.

Other speech and/or language disorders; -the boy, or his / her family for stuttering, expressed anxiety/fear.

Sadly, there is no independent factor or single predictor to assess or support an SLP to determine the likelihood that the children will start stuttering. The combination of all the data obtained helps determine the best treatment and course of action to be taken at this stage to reduce or provide effective intervention for children and/or adults.

Treatments for Stutter Calming: The diagnosis of a Stutter focuses more on mental causes than medical reasons because a stutter is not reduced or eliminated. Treatment will focus on skills and techniques to assist the person in managing his or her disorder and improving his oral communication. For instance, the SLP can teach the person to control his / her breathing. Calming breathes the person to feel relaxed by reducing anxiety that is often expressed while speaking. We will also learn how to monitor and control their speed. Through slowing speech levels and patterns, they also communicate in their sentences with less fluidity. In addition, they are instructed and observed as they learn to compile fewer words, which allows them to flow the words they try to elicit more smoothly. It takes time and patience for diagnosis. The person may need to seek treatment on a regular, weekly, or monthly basis, and monitoring will be vital to ongoing achievements.

The fact that people who stutter are already clinically conscious of their inability to express themselves to others without stress or anxiety is significant. But did you know that there are things people hearing the stutter often do which make them more painfully aware of their problem than ever? Of example, completing sentences or filling in the blanks means that speaking becomes more distracting when you become conscious of the impatience you have for your argument to complete; interrupting your thought is also something to be avoided because it is harder for you to make a statement when you can focus on what you want to say. Individuals who want to be treated with fair respect and consideration as any other citizen give them the time to produce what they want to say and listen patiently. Not make statements like "take time," or "calm down," "take a deep breath," because that too makes it harder for them to focus, as it contributes to more anger and anxiety and often contributes to their inability to complete their sentence without further stuttering.

Individuals who work together with SLPs should create their approaches so that they will connect at a level where they feel more comfortable and secure. It is helpful to ask the person how they (the listener) want you to respond while talking. It is essential to interact frequently with an individual who is struggling with stuttering. Letting the person know that they are interested in "what" and not "how" will certainly reduce their fear, stress, and embarrassment. "I don't want you to feel uncomfortable interacting with me, so please let me know how you want me to answer when and/or when you are stuttering." That statement should be made in a non-collusion way that provides the individual with the trust and sincerity needed for talking with you, since he/she may stumble on certain words.

Although the exact cause of stuttering is unknown, studies indicate that genetics can play an important role. It may be the human inherited traits that have contributed to a stutter, owing to the inability that one can create sentences, partially because of the incapacity to regulate different muscle movements. Whatever the underlying reason, it makes communication difficult for many affected by the disorder. In this regard, we need to understand how we can support vs. how we hurt to relieve the anger, humiliation, and anxiety that go hand-in-hand with issues of speech development.

Are You Building Bridges of Communication with Your Children?

How does a child become a healthy and responsible adult? One who takes up challenges, recovers from difficulties, and develops positive and close relationships with others? Anyone? Anyone? The solution has always been confirmed. When only one responsible person is caring for a child, the child's ability to develop into a successful adult increase exponentially. Guess what? Guess what? You, Mom and Dad, are responsible, loving parents!

When a child has a healthy relationship with a responsible adult, she knows that she has someone to support, guide, and console her. It gives her the opportunity to explore the world. If a child knows that he can make mistakes and learn from them, he knows that somebody in his corner understands and endorses him. It gives him the strength to recover and try again. That's why it's important to create a safe relationship with your child by establishing bridges to your heart and mind rather than building a wall that damages your relationship-and your child.

Don't wait to wake you up from a crisis! Know the warning signs of walls being erected.

There are a variety of signs that your parenting with your child may need some research. You will break this wall down before it is too high by keeping your eyes and ears open for these possible clues.

You are building walls, warning signs.

Your child has little self-esteem or needful or clinging behavior.

A child who has low self-esteem is likely to be timid or overly hostile. He or she can easily be upset by criticism, still, try to make others happy. This child may not easily let go if he believes he has no safe haven to return.

Your child is uncontrolled or susceptible to stinging.

If a child does not know how to get to or around her home, it only seems that through impulsive actions, she can achieve her goals. Temperatures will happen if the child does not know any other way to communicate.

Your child has trouble in school or with peers.

Your child may have trouble with grades or find it difficult to know. He may also have difficulty making friends or communicating with friends efficiently.

Your child is sad, apathetic, or food-loving.

When a child is sad or apathetic, she thinks that she doesn't control things and is helpless in her life. Nutrition may be an excuse to feel bad and a cure for problems.

There are many ways a parent can establish a stable relationship with a child. Such strategies are called "bridges" since they cover the gap between you and your favorite child.

Building Bridges Contact your child with affection, admiration, and respect.

Recall when you fell in love the first time? You wanted to share it all with your loved one. And that love made him feel safe in sharing it with you. One of the first steps to build bridges is to love your child. Make a list of the attributes you appreciate and admire the wonderful child who is calling you mother or father!

Be there and work together to solve your children's problems.

You have to provide a haven for her as a parent to share her problems. This creates a sense of security and confidence that will help her to solve problems. And if she comes to you, let her come up with possible solutions, so try them alone. That's how she learns to make good choices in life.

Listen, listen, hear, and let your child understand you.

The number one ability to build connections, communicate and settle disputes between parents and children listens to the point of view of the other person. That doesn't mean that you will always agree, but you want to build a bridge that is meaningful to your child.

Spend one-on-one time together.

While it may be hard to work on your timetable, your child will learn that you appreciate spending time with him by playing games, chatting, baking, or planning an event. So booting will be enjoyable for you.

Do not worry about perfection. Perfection.

It's essential to build a safe bond, not just for your kids, but also for you. You're happiest when you feel close to your baby. This connection will set the stage together for the rest of your lives. It's time to build these bridges and make that connection!

Did you also know that a form of commendation could lead to self-defeating behavior and anxiety, while another could lead your children to positive actions? Adding a few words will make a difference in your child's life at night and day.

Chapter Five: Child Anxiety Treatment

Suppose your mind unites, there are skies to explore. The dialog often takes place: if minds are divided against one another, there is a sort of fear that seizes and does not release the unconscious human. The time that this type of behavior is triggered varies from person to person. We that meet some people here and there who also have rapid mood changes that intensify the state of anxiety. To know how to fix it, it is crucial to understand that child anxiety therapy will inevitably become simpler. First, it becomes a problem to eliminate the surrounding distress signals. The understanding of cognitive behavior is necessary. You may not manifest it in itself as a separate facet; you may not present the changes in irrational behavior as something concrete but rather make reason the irrational component. In speech therapies and interactive sessions, when recognition stops behind common things and processes, this can be easily recognized. Helping the child recognize how one reacts to the two different things will help him to conclude how to view the problem in perspective.

Acceptance Commitment Therapy is a child anxiety therapy that is helpful in stress relief. It is very helpful how spontaneity is produced to make people realize themselves and their actions. Therapy Dialectical Behavioral (DBT) is used for people who can take care of behavioral aspects. The tasks should be raised slowly without stressing or ignoring the performance.

Fear is now recognized as a state of mind where physicality is in immediate disharmony with the person's actions or sentiments. Once you reconcile the person with the emotions and through the physicality, the person begins to overcome their fear by himself. If you have trouble doing it on your own, you need to attend other group interaction sessions to reassure you that the problem you face is not special. They will then have the confidence to face the problem themselves.

In the first case, the separation between real life and imagination is a problem for some. This can be caused by medicines used to cure some other medical condition or by inherited forms of disability. In rare circumstances, the illness may be caused by a shock or injury in which the patient becomes severely disturbed and often finds the recovery difficult. Most adults can handle the situation themselves. However, the child still has to understand the truth from a wider perspective, and thus the problem is severe.

Nobody wants their child to live anxiously and fearfully. But it's a part of life to deal with difficult and stressful circumstances. If a child doesn't learn how to deal with anxiety effectively as he grows up, he will have problems of a lifetime. Since untreated anxiety can affect someone's entire life, it is crucial to treat child anxiety appropriately. A parent needs to take action before anxiety becomes a habit.

Children have difficulties handling their emotions, so their strong emotions are often played out. Each child answers differently. A child may become violent when anxiety hits. Or they might get discouraged. Or they can turn to their parents in search of support. Or they can cling and withdraw. Again, the answer is as personal as a child.

Part of growing up is learning to manage anxiety-generating personal or social situations. If you believe that your child has anxiety behavior, part of your job as a parent is to guide them about how they can deal with anxiety properly without acting or suppressing their emotions. This is an outstanding job. It's critical. Here is an idea that you can try and help your child with emotions and anxiety.

Young kids don't abstractly think. For them, the word "anxiety" has little meaning as a concept. All children are experts in facial expressions, however. This allows you to use images in a book or magazine to help children become more emotionally expert.

For example, you may collect the photos of happy kids, and then sit down with your child, asking questions like "What do you think the boy feels like?" "Why do you think he felt like this?" "What do you think he thinks he's thinking?"

Then you can see photos of children who seem nervous and ask questions about them. The child can answer questions about the anxious child in the picture in such a way that certain items that bother you show. Even if this isn't happening, you can ask your kid what the worried child can do to feel better in the picture. You can use the discussion to suggest possible solutions for your child. Maybe you could say something like, "If I was that boy and concerned about myself, I think I should talk about that with mom and dad.

Child Psychology - Understanding Children

Child psychology must be based on the understanding of each child's sensitivity. We are very reactive when we are children because our organism is still growing. They are too naive. Too stupid. Everything can, therefore, have a very negative effect on our psychological development.

You start to understand your children when you study child psychology and, at the same time, begin to understand yourself. You note the significance of many specifics for our personality development. You know what is essential to a child and much more.

Unresected and neglected children develop serious psychological problems from the outset of their schooling. If you've had a sad childhood, you'll probably have many psychological issues, even if you don't know their presence or other behavioral changes.

You must be extremely careful if you are a parent so that you can always demonstrate to your child that you love him or her.

For your children to be healthy and self-confident, you must: Be very gentle with each child and be cautious about their problems. Any time you show your anger to him, he concludes that' daddy or mommy doesn't love me.'

A child can not understand that his / her questions are stupid, or that you tire of working too much to feed your family. Even when you have no patience to answer his questions or to fix his broken toy, a child can not understand that you still love him greatly.

Of course, even when they noise, you just love your kids and want to get rid of them. You never cease to love your kids.

But a child doesn't know this fundamental truth.

They will simply conclude that you don't love them if you don't give all your attention to your children. We can't show understanding. We are too naive and highly egotistical. Your kids believe that all your energy must be focused all the time. You can't respect your exhaustion. You can not understand the seriousness of the problems you face, because you have many obligations and you stop making stupid requests.

Certain children understand the problems of their parents, and some even help their parents in all ways. These children are rare, however. Most children are completely indifferent to the concerns of their parents.

In a very simple and direct way, children think. We have not yet established their logic. You must recall your childhood to understand your children.

You will return to the past when you have children and' grow up with them,' as if you were re-growing. You can understand many things about your creation as you continue to develop them, allowing you to understand your reactions.

Try to remember how you felt when your parents weren't doing what you wanted them to do. Kids aren't smart people. All that's wrong for them is the end of the world. You must always note that they are extremely sensitive, greedy (actually self-centered), and ignorant.

• Never use violence-Even if many people believe that' only' parents can threaten their children with violence until now; this is the worst mistake you can make. If you are violent with your children while they are too young, for this reason, they would hate you. They will later become violent teenagers, and their actions can ruin your life.

The consequences of abuse are even worse than you can imagine. All mental illnesses are linked to our childhood psychological problems.

You must always give your children love, patience, and understanding, and support them in every way. Talk to your children. Talk to your children. Explain what's dangerous and bad. Give them more lectures. Show them more lessons. Open their eyes. Open their eyes. Help them learn to live. Support them.

Always show love— Even for many reasons, you have to swallow your pain, always be kind and compassionate with each child, even if you're tired, sad, or angry.

For an infant, love is more important than anything else. Even if you can't give them enough food, you'll still be a good parent if you show them your love.

Therefore, don't believe that you will owe them' your love' by buying whatever your children want. Love is not material. Love is not material. You must give all your attention and affection to your children. If:* Hug them warmly* Frequently hug them* Listen* Answer all their questions, you can still be concerned that you really don't know what to do. Which counselor are you supposed to follow?

The wise unconscious mind that creates your visions and has a spiritual basis is the greatest psychologist you can find. The importance of dreams combines science and religion.

Dream translation by the scientific method discovered and condensed by Carl Jung will help you to understand the insightful direction of your dreams in the unconscious. The unconscious mind that creates the visions is wise and holy and acts as a natural physician. This offers free psychotherapy in all dream photos and scenes.

Every dream picture contains important messages that help you to achieve balance. You have information on the psychological reality of your children as well. The unconscious mind is very generous and gives you precious knowledge and advice on everything you need.

You will also be able to translate the essence of dreams using the right method, translate the dreams of your children, and understand several things you never would otherwise know.

Carl Jung had been a genuine genius. My work shows that his theories have been true discoveries. You will be fascinated by all the knowledge you have when you know the dream language in your dreams.

I will translate your dreams for you if you need urgent help. You will later learn the dream language when you have time and the ability to do so.

The unconscious mind will teach you how to perceive the responses of your child and to value his or her personality rather than to force your will. This is another very great danger to which you have to pay attention. Many parents tend to impose on their children a certain action without paying attention to their characteristics.

Everyone inherits, because everyone is born, the fundamental attributes of his personality to a certain psychological type, as Carl Jung may find after a long time of serious research. Nevertheless, this finding has never been accepted by the world; not all psychologists and psychiatrists have acknowledged it until now.

Psychology is a field with many different consequences. Each psychologist uses his method or another psychologist's method. In this area, there are no basic rules.

Nevertheless, my findings after Carl Jung's work into the mysterious area of the human psyche through dream interpretation prove to the world that everyone will definitely study jung's dream interpretation approach. Everybody must also accept the presence of psychological characteristics that define human behavior, especially because they are unilateral and cause neurosis.

Now that we know that the Jung approach actually communicates the essence of the unconscious vision, and now that we know the healing power of dreams, we need dream therapy to avoid all mental illness. All psychologists and psychiatrists need to learn the dream interpretation method of Carl Jung to help their patients with this knowledge. All persons must learn this knowledge; it must be taught in all schools.

The unconscious mind is the universe's greatest therapist and psychologist. The unconscious experience would help humanity eradicate all mental disorders characterizing the human race fully.

You should always remember that you have to respect the psychological type of your child without imposing your opinion or distorting its personality. In this task, your unconscious mind will help you by sending you many dreams about the personality of your child and your personality.

To you, I condensed Carl Jung's system. Now you can quickly learn how to interpret the essence of dreams instantly. The vocabulary of dreams today is not a mystery.

The theoretical interpretations of the interpretation of your dreams help you to understand and appreciate your children clearly. You will raise happy kids, happy teenagers, and happy adults.

You will also undergo a psychotherapy and mental development process. You will, therefore, become a relaxed and balanced person. You can also translate the meaning of the dreams of your husband and wife in the same way that you translate the meaning of the dreams of your children.

The vocabulary of the vision is always the same. Based on the dreamer, the meaning does not change, as many incorrect dream interpreters believe. This means that only once in your life, you have to study this language. Then you will always have the implicit encouragement, guiding you in every way.

Children and Generalized Anxiety Disorder

Many anxiety disorders affect women, usually beginning with puberty. One of the few common anxiety disorders that also affects children. Children who suffer from pervasive anxiety are constantly worried about everything, their families, education, school problems, and world events, to name a few. You worry so much that it takes so many years to mess with your ability to function and do what most average children do. If this sounds like your son, his doctor will have him checked out. Other health problems can be the same, and the doctor will have to be sure that you administer the correct treatment. Worry for more than six months is a pretty good indicator of the common anxiety disorder.

Children suffering from generalized anxiety disorder suffer from several other symptoms such as restlessness or failure to concentrate, sleep failure, often extremely tiredness, and often very irritable.

Families play a major role in helping kids learn how to handle their generalized anxiety disorder so that their daily lives may not interfere. These children respond well to positive methods of parenting and always seek to reassure themselves that everything is all right. Families will try to assist their children by speaking about their fears and concerns and showing them how irrational they are.

If a severe anxiety disorder is not properly treated before puberty, a whole new set of problems may arise. Children can suffer from self-esteem and problems of confidence, may never graduate, can not join the workforce, and may turn to alcohol or medicines to make them feel better.

Children with widespread anxiety disorder typically react well to treatments such as cognitive behavior. Cognitive behavior therapy teaches children to change their thinking and to change their behavior to reduce fears and concerns. This allows them to become confident about their negative thoughts and actions. Students learn about using relaxation exercises to control their stress so that they can handle their condition more effectively. Children need to learn to use these forms of calming, not just in therapy, but at any time and anywhere in stressful situations.

You need to look for a therapist that is easy to communicate and who has no problem answering questions that you may have when choosing to help your child with his generalized anxiety disorder. He should be able to tell you everything you want to know about his education, his treatment, and how much you should expect to pay for it all.

You might want to conduct interviews with several clinicians specializing in treating children with generalized anxiety disorders before making your final choice. Feel free to ask questions during your interview to help you make the best choice for your child. It is a good idea to ask prospective therapists how long they have used generalized anxiety disorder to treat children, and how long have they been qualified to do so. Ask what happens during an average treatment session and learn how long each session will last. Can parents sit in the sessions? How many procedures does it usually take to be improved? You should also find out if your insurance covers the therapist, and if not, if he is prepared to prepare a payment plan with you to make the treatment for the family budget easier for your child. Let your child also visit possible counselors to see whether he or she likes each other.

You may also want to study each potential therapist after you interview multiple therapists to see if you find concerns or other data that helps you during the selection process. Choosing a counselor is not an easy task for your kid, and you should take the time to choose the right one.

While prescription medicines seem to support diagnosed with a generalized anxiety disorder, they are not all recommended for child use. Generally, best results are achieved by combining medications with psychological therapy. Use the drugs before psychological therapy works, then phase out the narcotics. It is not advisable for anyone, especially children, to use prescription anxiety medications for long periods. The doctor may be able to find a safe prescription medicine but note that some medications that are commonly used in adult treatments may cause children to have self-destructive thoughts and behavior. Kids who use medications to help control their common anxiety disorders should be closely monitored by both their doctor and family. The physician should be immediately notified of new symptoms or changes in personality.

People with generalized anxiety disorders might well later in life develop other psychiatric diseases, such as chronic depression or panic disorders. Treatment and counseling at the outset of a generalized anxiety disorder will reduce the odds considerably.

Symptoms of Child Anxiety

Parents can come to help children fight separation anxiety. A child sees his home as his true refuge, and the concept of home comfort is born. He is not prepared for a changing environment that is largely alien to him most of the time. This sudden separation from home comfort creates a form of social anxiety called separation anxiety. Families may be the first part of the treatment for separation anxiety.

If a parent provides help, love, and security and simultaneously rationally prepares a child for the imminent separation, he provides half of the separation anxiety treatment. It is also crucial to intimate teachers with certain commitments for children, for example, school pick-up time. Thus, children are led to believe that the parents mean what they say and are guaranteed that any separation will culminate in time.

Separation concerns are largely present in the early years because children only really understand and want to stick with a parent-child relationship permanently. This relationship is their defense against suffering; this relationship is their watch over time. Over time you begin to grasp the nuances of other relationships and become more confident individuals. Separation Anxiety Therapy is, therefore, most prominent during childhood.

Besides that, separation anxiety therapy in children can be handled by getting babysitters and caregivers at any time o Simulating separation to desensitize a child o Unfamiliar surroundings o Telling a child we will return when we leave A child can become traumatized in his early years because his brain is not conditioned to accept changes. This can lead to persistent mental cavities. It is, therefore, essential that the above lines of separation anxiety therapy are followed.

Child anxiety attacks are fairly common, the exact number of patients is nevertheless unknown, probably because the condition is often under-diagnosed or simply not reported. It is treatable with good medical care, but experts say that when childhood anxieties are left untreated, they are more likely to manifest themselves in an adult mental disorder. Briefly, taking the steps needed to treat childhood anxiety attacks will help reduce the chances of adult anxiety.

Below are some signs and symptoms of kid anxiety so that you can see if your child has an anxiety disorder.

Generalized anxiety disorder or GAD is described by fear or persistent uncertainty about anything and all for no logical reason. The signs of the childhood of GAD are very similar to the adult version. GAD patients may complain of exhaustion, stomach upset, sleeping problems, and restlessness. Even the child can cry, throw tantrums, hyped up, have bad dreams, and even begin to experience school problems.

Separation Anxiety is a very common problem for children as they reach school age. You will show signs of panic and fear that you are separated from your home and your family. Symptoms may include crying and not going to school. The child may also complain of an illness that would normally keep him or her out of school. Alternatively, the child can show an attitude at home or in the parents ' company.

You have social phobia, almost the opposite of separation anxiety. A socially phobic child can choose to stay at home. It will remain away because it feels like it doesn't fit in or because it is afraid of being humiliated in public. You choose to stay at home and watch TV or read a book rather than go out and mix.

You get performance anxiety closely linked to social anxiety. A child with math and reading difficulties can become ill and panicked if he or she is called on to do something before the whole class. They can also show signs of fear when they are not very good at sports.

So, what triggers child anxiety?

There are several ways in which children can become anxious. Evidence has shown that children with nervous parents are more likely to be anxious. A child can also develop anxiety when it is raised by parents that are perfectly normal. They can develop anxiety because of a bad experience. Being a victim of bullying, humiliation, and mockery of their fellow students are all childhood-related problems that can lead to anxiety. Also, family problems include the death of a family member or close friend, the separation of parents, abuse, or any trauma. Finally, a personal phobia is like fearing the dark, fearing being alone and fear of certain animals.

If your child has childhood anxiety symptoms, they may be the same as a variety of other medical problems, often much worse than depression. It is very vital that you bring your child to the doctor so that he or she can get the correct treatment he or she wants.

Most have at least a dose of childhood anxiety during childhood, so it isn't a great problem. Since your child shows what you think is child anxiety, I strongly advise you to get the best advice and help. Deep knowledge will, in every way, help you.

There are many types of anxiety. The most common symptoms of anxiety are panic disorder, generalized anxiety, and OCD, although OCD may result from a non-treated problem.

A child will display under pressure any of the following-

- Sleep pattern modifications?

- Maybe bedwetting?

- Sleepwalking?

- Walking? Change / Appetite loss?

- Is your child calmer than normal?

- Personality change or misbehavior?

- Wouldn't you like to go to school today ... again?

- A sudden "affliction" under a given circumstance?

Please note that a child is not going to recognize such feelings of anxiety and symptoms, so emphasize the symptoms more and don't the cause.

Panic disorder was the most popular symptom of childhood anxiety. It is characterized by repeated, chronic, unalerted panic attacks. These include fear and physical symptoms very unpleasant. You will experience some of the following.

- choking,

- dizziness,

- shortness of breath,

- nausea,

- numbness in the hands or feet,

Modified sense of reality and sense of environmental alienation symptoms:

- chest pain,

- trembling or shaking,

- sweating,

- Pounding heart,

The recommended treatments need to be carefully monitored. Anxiety-based disorders disrupt the ability of children to live normal lives. The anxiety symptoms may be harmful, if not checked.

Chapter Six: Social Anxiety and Phobia - A Remnant Of Trauma genic Family Dynamics

A very talented engineer sought help in the last few months with a difficult problem that interfered almost every day in his professional life. She had been in the same industry for seven years and was very active in small projects. Because of her talents and skills, she was promoted not only to run an office of this major company but also to manage an entire division of the company. At this point, when her problems started to trick in, she had to travel a lot, mainly regionally, and address groups of other professionals, contractors, and those seeking services via her organization at medium to large meetings (12-50 participants).

It would be normal in such changing circumstances that most people would feel nervous from time to time, but it became devastatingly anxious and conscious of itself. She began to avoid situations as far as possible, and she felt the following when she could not avoid them:-Blurry and becoming very red in the face and neck-Profuse sweating, to make her dress visibly damp as it had been rained upon.

Trembling or shaking-nauseous or even vomiting-stomach upheaval and extreme stomach acid-trouble in speaking without stuttering, chocking, and rapid breathing-weak voice and difficulty with pitch or sound-muscle tension so severe that her body was physically aching as if she had exercised intensely.

She experienced social anxiety or social phobia that is usually called a strong and persistent fear of being scrutinized, judged, and found to be lacking or to do something embarrassing that might call other people's skills into question. Being unbelievably luminous and quite logical, it was a difficult situation to contend with this young woman as she knew that she had both irrational and negative fears and that the more she addressed them in her mind, the greater and more ingrained they became.

The repeated experiences of that talented young woman went something like this: anxiety before the encounter, where she would worry about and imagine all possible scenarios that could be catastrophic, go badly wrong or badly reflect on her or her company. With every new scenario, she realized that there were many and painful possibilities that generated rising emotional distress. With three to four days before most large meetings, she could create enough emotional and physical distress to become physically ill.

She found it difficult to focus or not to get lost during presentations when providing information and organizing the delivery and answering questions from the attendants.

Subsequently, worry about how her performance was measured and imagine some of the negative and unflattering stuff that those present have to say about her and her skills.

Who causes social or phobia anxieties?

There is a common misconception that social anxiety or phobia begins in teenage years and that it's an unfortunate experience of being a nervous or awkward teenager. Some writers even point to childhood and say that "shy" kids mature to socially anxious adults. But the reality is sometimes, if not much more complicated than those reductions.

Not only this young woman, who is particularly talented, but many who suffer worsening anxiety and social phobia are raised in environments where family dynamics disrupted or affected by normal mental, emotional, and social growth. These family dynamics are collectively referred to as stressful family dynamics and lie at the heart of this complex condition. Imagine yourself as a child raised in an environment in which safety, security, stability, empathy, and acceptance are sometimes available but not predictable or consistent. Where the dynamic family may be characterized as detached, cool, or unpredictable, those who "must" love you often show instability or unreliability.

Typical development of this stressful family dynamic is an all-embracing feeling that one is in essential respects incomplete, evil, lower, or invalid. Sometimes children learn to be hypersensitive to criticism, to reject, to become extremely conscious, making continuous comparisons between a certain unobtainable ideal and themselves. Traumatic dynamics of the family can lay the stage and lay the foundations for a child to adopt and believe that they are significantly defective and will inevitably fail, or fundamentally inadequate in fields of achievement compared to their peers. Often it includes assumptions that one is dumb, incompetent, untalented and stupid, and many of the following symptoms that lead: -Intense fear that you may not know people or feel smarter, better educated, or more effective in situations.

Fear of circumstances in which you can be evaluated, measured, hidden, or attacked in any way.

A permanent and pervasive worry about embarrassing or humiliating yourself –anxiety which disturbs your everyday routine, work, school, or other activities, either by absorbing thought through possible disaster scenarios or by confusing you with general principles of how to perform your tasks to a very low degree.

Avoid doing things or speak out people out of fear of ridicule, ignoring circumstances where you are, could be at the center of attention, -Extreme difficulties in promoting you or your abilities even when you're extraordinarily talented. Many of these wealthy and smart people struggle with all-pervading feelings of worthlessness or self-esteem and struggle to become self-assertive in most working and personal relationships. The sufferer often has a gargoyle-like an inner critic, weeping negative messages and malicious allegations, often weakly referred to as negative self-interest, and a profound fear and logical hypersensitivity.

So, what is it possible to do?

The first challenge is treatment by understanding that many people have created a life to prevent situations that cause social anxiety reactions due to the nature of their developmental background and stressful family dynamics and that many sufferers will only seek treatment when their ability to adapt and handle their lives is overwhelmed by it. Often doctors are initially prescribing a variety of medicines that can ease the symptoms, but not provide permanent or necessary relief.

Cognitive-compatible therapy helps the patient recognize injunctions (rules) that create fear and serve as corrosion agents on an individual's identity or self-esteem; or guidance that tends to be the most helpful outcomes with a social anxiety disorder. CBT also helps to identify the patterns and causes that cause anxiety for a person.

Enhancement of relationships and training of social skills. This therapy helps you to develop your skills in social situations by practicing and playing roles. The depression is growing when you are relaxed and ready for the social situations that are feared.

Cognitive reorganization. Such counseling offers the client the resources for better and more accurate control of their thought rather than reactive anxiety and concern learning.

Child Maltreatment - Effects on Brain Development and Behavior

Neglect, physical abuse, and sexual exploitation (widely called child abuse) have a significant and long-term impact on a child's development, and their effects on child development, brain development, psychopathology, and interpersonal relationships. With higher rates of psychological distress, elevated incidence of substance abuse, and several serious relationship problems, a child's long-term effects of prolonged early treatment (also called Complex Post Traumatic Stress Disorder) can be seen. Child abuse is an intergenerational problem. The perpetrators of abuse and neglect are most often deeply damaged people who are abused and neglected.

Clear connections exist between neglect and abuse and subsequent psychological, behavioral, interpersonal, and emotional disorders. The basis of this connection is the impact of abuse and neglect on brain development.

We recognize that a child uses the mind of the parent to control the mental processes of the infant. The child creates self-regulation skills, emotional control, behavioral management, and cognitive capacities as a cause-effect approach amongst others through a sensitive, attentive, and caring relationship with a primary care provider. The development of a child's ability to regulate emotions and to develop a coherent sense of self requires sensitive and responsive parenthood. The National Adoption Center has determined that 52% of adopted children have symptoms of attachment disorder. In another study, 80 percent of maltreated or abused infants exhibited symptoms of attachment disorder by Cicchetti, & Barnett. The best predictor for a child's annexation classification is the state of mind regarding the annexation of the birth mother. A classification of an attachment of a mother before the birth of her child can predict the attachment classification of her child at six years of age with 80 percent accuracy. This is an excellent result. Finally, a recent study by Maria Dozier, PhD, shows that the foster mother's attachment classification has a profound effect on the child's attachment classification. She found that after three months of employment, the classification of the attachment of the child is similar to that of the foster mother. These findings argue strongly for a non-genetic mechanism for transmitting attachment patterns over generations.

The risk of sexually exploited adolescence is high (2.0 times the average), major depressive disorders (3.4 times the average), alcohol abuse (2.5 times the average), drug abuse (3.8 times the average), and anti-social behavior (4.3 times the average)

Generally, the left hemisphere of the brain is the center of speech, right-hand motor movement, and language-based logical thinking. The right brain hemisphere is responsible for left body motor activity, context perceptions, face recognition, interpersonal and emotional treatment, and holistic perception. In the brain's prefrontal lobes, the orbital-frontal cortex (a part of the brain directly behind the eyes) is responsible for integrating emotional responses that are produced within the limbic system with higher cognitive functions, including planning and language. The left orbitofrontal cortex is responsible for creating a memory and the right orbit-frontal cortex for retrieving the memory. The healthy activity requires a right and left hemisphere to be incorporated. During the first year of life, a significant number of synaptic connections between brain cells grow into the middle of the second year of life. An integrated brain requires connections of the corpus callosum between hemispheres. Children abused and neglected have a less corpus callosum than children who are unamused. Children who are abused and neglected have poorly integrated brain hemispheres. This lack of integration of the hemisphere and the underdevelopment of the cortex are the foundation of symptoms such as the difficulty in regulating the emotion, lack of thinking about causes, inability of emotions in others to be recognized accurately, the child's inability to articulate his own emotions, autobiographical history and an incoherent sense of self, and lack of awareness.

Mistreated children's brains are not as well integrated as unamused kids ' brains. This helps to explain why children maltreated have serious emotional regulation, integrated functioning, and social development difficulties. The development of consciousness and empathy is largely a function of the orbitofrontal cortex. There are major social and emotional difficulties when development in this area of the brain is hindered. It is very interesting that the cortex is sensitive to face and eye contact. Maltreated children often experience attachment disorders because their parents do not have sensitive reaction interactions with the child.

Early interpersonal interactions have a profound effect on the brain, as brain circuits that incorporate social cognition functions like generating context, controlling the body state, regulating emotion, organizing memory and interpersonal interaction, and empathy are similar. Stressing interactions that actively traumatize or cause chronic elevated neuroendocrine hormone levels. High levels of these hormones will permanently damage the memory of the hippocampus. On this basis, we can conclude that psychological trauma can affect the ability of a person to build and maintain memory and prevent the resolution of trauma.

Abused and neglected children have a variety of actions that can contribute to several diagnoses. In several important areas of development, however, the impact of early abuse and neglect on the child can be seen. These include emotional regulation, behavioral regulation, attachment, biology, flexibility in response, a coherent, integrated feeling of self over time, the capacity to interact with significant people (empathy and emotional connection), self-conception, cognitive skills, and learning and development of consciences.

Early mistreatment has significant and lasting effects on the development of a child. It is the impact of abuse on the brain of a child that results in effects, including social, psychological, and cognitive development. The ability to regulate and emotionally associate feelings with others relies on early experiences and the formation of different areas of the brain. Early abuse causes deficits in brain development, mainly in orbitofrontal corpus and cortex callosum, due to the toxic influences of stress hormones on the development brain.

Such results strongly indicate that effective treatment involves an affectively reactive relationship. Siegel said: "As parents reflect with their children securely on the mental conditions which create a shared subjective experience, they are joined by a crucial co-constructive process to understand how the mind works. The inherent feature of a safe attachment-of contingent collaborative communication-is also a fundamental part of how interpersonal relationships function. For example, when the customer in a therapeutic relationship focuses on aspects of traumatic memory and feels the consequences of those memories without getting dysregulated, the customer gains an improved capacity to withstand increasing amounts of harm. The customer learns to regulate himself. The well-tuned relationship between the patient and the psychologist makes sense (the role of the Left-Hemisphere) from memories, autobiographical perceptions, and experiences (the function of the right-hemisphere).

Children with Separation Anxiety

Anxiety about separation is relatively common. Separation anxiety may appear in different situations such as school or daycare.

Kids get on the school bus.

Going to bed upstairs while Mama and Dad are downstairs is difficult to know with absolute certainty, the root cause of such distress. We are, however, aware that several different circumstances can help children with anxiety about separation.

1. Increased anticipatory anxiety contributes to the anxiety of separation.

If a child has a stressful time due to changes in classes, relationships, families, parents, or any other occurrence that raises their overall anxiety, then it would be a moment when they would be more vulnerable to separating fears.

2. The more... the far more vulnerable.

Families over-protect children without being saved from these upheavals have not been allowed to experience upheaval. This is one of the hallmarks of the overprotected child, and parents unintentionally nurture a weaker sense of self-esteem and trust.

3. Parents who react overreact to the anxiety of their children promote anxiety about separation.

Some parents are susceptible to their child's emotional reactions. When your child gets upset, it tends to impute emotional distress that matches what an adult will feel.

This is simply not correct and leads parents to over-react to their children's slightest upheavals.

4. Significant disturbance or mistrust in parental relationships.

Throughout separation and divorce, the bond between a child and a parent may be significantly affected for legal or logistical reasons. When children feel a deep loss or fear of a permanent loss with their parents, they can start to compute.

5. When parents let the fear of adults become the fear of their children.

If parents fear their children "can't handle it," they often tell their children about it. You don't do it directly... you do it with your emotional reactions and voice tone. You do so with the questions you ask. They do so in the way they constantly test and ask about the experiences of a child.

What can parents do about anxiety over separation?

1) Don't medicate your children.

I saw this disappointment over and over again. This is not a situation in which children need medication. It's not the problem's root.

They don't make up their emotions. It's just that they've come to believe that they can't handle something they can do. Medicines only grow to be a crutch, and ultimately their anxiety increases as the child's environment continues to work to strengthen their anxiety.

2) Get out your child's feelings.

Make sure that your fears and concerns have not become the fears and worries of your son. Whether you worry about them going to school or how they will deal with situations after a breakup, this fear, and depression, you have to contend with yourself.

Don't carry these feelings into discussions with your children, because they have reason to be frightened and worried.

3) Start to believe... "They can do it!" This is a simple and plain reality. Your child may go to school. Your child may be left in daycare. Your child should take care of going into the house of dad... Or go back to the house of Mom.

Your boys can do it. Hold that always in your mind. You will be surprised to learn how your actions and beliefs form your children's underlying beliefs. The more you give them the confidence that they can handle what they really have to do... The sooner their depression disappears.

4) Make short and sweet transitions.

The most serious mistake you can make is a long time off. The second major mistake is to ask many preparatory questions and to provide an enormous explanation (again and again) before a transition happens.

Both will certainly lead to failure because they express the feeling of confusion as to whether or not your child will cope with this.

5) Do not commit (repeated) upsets.

This is known to every elementary and daycare teacher. When your child goes to the classroom and begins to sob, they ask you to leave quickly. Everything is well in five minutes, and life goes on.

This teacher learned that they couldn't continue giving the upset a lot of energy. If they do, the upheaval becomes worse. Then, they turn your child to the other kids and go away.

Medications for children with anxiety disorders depend mostly on your child's type of anxiety disorder. Choosing the right treatment is crucial for a thorough cure for anxiety disorder. First, before choosing treatment, you need to know what kind of anxiety disorder your child has. My childhood Diagnosis of Anxiety Disorder can be useful to decide what kind of anxiety disorder your child has.

If you know the type of anxiety disorder your child has clearly and accurately, you can read the blow to find out the treatment that your child needs.

1. Generalized Anxiety Disorder Treatment

Children are suffering from overly serious concerns and fears about various events, including the past, present, and future generalized anxiety disorder (also called

GAD). Generalized anxiety disorder Most times, high anxiety interferes with childhood and casual relationships.

To cure this type of disorder, parents or caretakers can use several treatment methods, including educating the children about the nature of anxiety and ways of identifying, evaluating, and changing anxiety. This method can be complemented by relaxation strategies training.

Teaching children with Generalized Anxiety Disorder to understand the physical symptoms of anxiety can also be a successful method. In this method, positive self-talk can be encouraged instead of negative. The parents should offer rewards and prizes for the success of their son.

2. *Panic Disorder Treatment*

Panic disorders are one of the most life-threatening anxiety disorders. Repeated attacks of panic characterize them. The repeated episodes of panic attacks lead to concern and concern for the sufferers. Individuals with panic disorders appear to discourage themselves from going out or engaging in circumstances that caused them to panic.

Panic attacks include an episode of terrible thoughts and physical symptoms such as a pounding heart that can not easily relax.

Most medications are available for anxiety and panic attacks.

Cognitive-behavioral therapy is one of the treatments widely used and highly regarded. This method is mainly used for adult patients, and the results show an increasing trend in treatment success. Cognitive behavior therapy teaches children to recognize and change negative thinking patterns to remove fear and worry about panic attack events. Patients will learn to identify negative thoughts that cause panic attacks automatically. This will allow patients to control their emotions and avoid their anxiety and panic from taking control of their minds.

Exposure therapy can be another method of treatment. In this counseling, children are taught advanced strategies and approaches to reduce their fear of anxiety and panic. Through counselors, children may enter environments that they previously avoided and learn to cope through their "bad thinking" and succeed.

3. Separation Anxiety Disorder

Separation anxiety disorder mainly occurs in younger children. The symptoms are unwilling to separate from parents or careers. The risk of separation from the comfort zone of children leads in large part to great distress and anxiety.

Cognitive compartmental therapy is one of the methods of treatment for this type of anxiety disorder. The method of therapy focuses on teaching children techniques in managing their anxiety and fear of separation. Children are taught to recognize and identify their anxiety-induced situations of separation. We are taught to develop strategies for dealing with these situations and to stop causing anxiety. Therefore, techniques such as modeling, role-playing, and relaxation learning. In addition, the cooperation of parents with the therapist in the healing process is considered extremely important and is well known to speed up treatment.

4. Phobia Treatment

Extraordinary and intense phobia children who have irrational roots suffer from a phobia. Things like escalators, bugs, aircraft, or situations like sleeping in the dark and walking to school can be the phobias. The people suffering from these events and circumstances will not know that terror has irrational origins. We would, therefore, be highly anxious and stressed if faced with the dreaded object or heart condition.

Cognitive-behavioral therapy of phobia is also used. Treatment methods can range from relaxation therapy, simulated use, and parental reinforcement. The tokens can be a variety of loves for stickers and diagrams. Children will also be taught to substitute better and more positive thoughts for their anxious and bad thoughts.

Exposure therapy is also used in the treatment of children with a phobia, which can be more useful than cognitive treatment. This method gradually introduces children to the situations that they fear. Of course, the qualified counselor should use this process.

Hypnotherapy could also help people to change and reprogram their subconscious patterns that usually form part of the phobia. The fears are minimized when the patterns that lead to phobia are fixed.

NLP can also be used for the treatment of phobia but is used mostly in adult patients. From the NLP's viewpoint, a phobia is the product of our programs or "constructions." Such systems don't really function well and cause problems in the lives of the patients. NLP aims to reprogram patients ' thinking patterns. This transforms the fearful thoughts into neutral thoughts. In the sense of its speed and effectiveness, NLP is helpful. Interventions and tests are easy to use and perform well.

5. Selective Mutism Treatment,

The special feature of selective mutism is the inability to speak about a particular social issue where speech is expected. This can happen in school with kids. Diagnosing someone with selective mutilation primarily means that a person is unable to interact with his or her social or academic life in a specific situation.

Professional physicians were mainly involved in the diagnosis of selective mutism. You start the treatment by trying to understand why, the source, and the causes of the issue. After the clinician has a clear understanding of the problem, the treatment continues with verbal mastery training. Other treatment devices can vary from role-playing to changing anxiety about speech. Relaxation techniques are also included in the patient's psychological arsenal.

Hands-on Science for Kids-Learn by Doing

You eat dinner, and your child is happy to describe how his teacher took a bucket of water and swung it around without a drop. Your child talks of centrifugal force! Your child's talking to you! My kid! Your child is amazed at this great experience he has had! Effective lessons give children good chances to talk! Children who can speak verbally to reinforce what they hear will improve their comprehension and memory. Current research suggests that, apart from conventional reading and listening approaches, children can electrify their imagination, offering memorable experiences and opportunities for debate! As parents, we already understand the value of "learning by doing" that allows our children to experience walking, talking, playing a game, or learning how to act.

Making deliberate decisions about what we teach our children has benefits well over the years. Families want what is best for their children, and, with the rise of technology-based industries, our children also need to gain knowledge and skills. Encouraging and supporting the interest of our children in science can help to balance their learning and curiosity. Activities that can form the basis and strengthen what children learn every day and reinforce their confidence.

Kids in grades 2, 3, and 4 will demonstrate an appreciation of magnetism, gravity, and light. Using one of the science packages, such as the ElectroWiz magnetism of ScienceWiz, Newton's Wizard, and WaveWiz Light, gives parents the chance to increase their children's understanding of scientific fundamentals.

What's in the future of your child? Maybe he'll help us find or refine a cleaner fuel source that will move us to a more sustainable future! The Fuel Cell Car-Research Kit from Thames &Kosmos is a fun research kit. Your child should learn how to build a green car and learn how to drive it through the ground using the power of the wind! Children will read and take part in ScienceWiz's Energy Wiz, a science pack. This kit teaches children about potential energy (energy stored pending use) and cinematic energy (energy used in the motion of an object). Build a solar racer to explore these concepts and test the differences between potential and cinematic capacity. Elenco's Solar Deluxe Educational Kit offers science education to help kids create solar models and produce renewable energy to power a radio or a device.

It is always a difficult task to encourage children to explore and question themselves. Encourage your child with a highly secret question. The Forensic Science Mystery Detective Kit is a sure way to make this fun and exciting way of thinking outside the box. Through studying DNA samples, identifying motivations, and other hints for minimizing the perpetrators and solving a mystery, children may overcome many mysteries. The Go Detective Science Kit will help children who might also learn from the mechanics of developing technology to investigate and prosecute crimes. Of 65 activities, children can use the microscope to make ink, learn Morse code, and analyze evidence. With one of several lenses and binoculars choices, it is easier to detect small hints—a great way to complete one of these unique science kits!

Electronics is a subject which flows through all areas of our lives. The Elenco Snap Circuits series starts with 100 (Junior) to Snap 300 and 500 Pro circuits. These unique science toys are great instruments that can help both children and adults to decrypt the electronics world through the introduction of some basic knowledge. Modules with resistors, condensers, and transistors simplify connections to integrate circuits and produce various effects. But if your child is ready for more realistic technology, consider Elenco's Create Your Telephone or Talking Clock Building Kit—both great ideas to bring children more deeply into science.

Seek a special science toy that can enable any astronaut or astronomer to start. Enlighten the imagination of your child with a motorized solar system. This imaginative science toy illuminates and shows the nature of the solar system. Teachers should build their planetarium for the classroom. The Solar System 3D Mobile Printing Kit is another cool science kit. Assemble the plastic planets, color your device using the included paint, and add them to your mobile phone-an an excellent home or classroom activity. All these science kits contain instructions and facts concerning our solar system.

Try the Usborne Book of Astronomy and Space for more detailed knowledge of the Universe, a perfect introduction to the wonders of space. Terence Dickinson's Exploration of the Night Sky is a great book that lets your children learn about the cosmos and provides an introduction to the stars. Mastermind also provides many powerful telescopes to inspire a star gasser in your family to look at the night sky

CONCLUSION

If your child is curious and excited but not scientifically motivated, you can perhaps persuade them with some odd science toys and kits. Remember the chemistry of Oobleck Gooey. Your child can now perform slimy experiments and begin a slime ooze competition as a teaching tool all around the world. Does the curiosity of your child in animals demand its full attention? The Fun With Your Dog Science Kit will satisfy your imagination by measuring the hearing of a dog, assessing the temperament of a dog, or creating dog bone cookies. Take advantage of Scientific Explorer's Spa Science Kit to the bathroom! Children can combine fragrances, make spray baths, and create smelling potions. Determine the difference between smells and family members and friends, the ultimate sensory test!

Science is a topic that permeates all areas of our lives; it is what you need to encourage curiosity and to learn to make it fun and interesting!

Made in the USA
Monee, IL
30 July 2021

74592954R00108